Shattered
But Not
Broken

A journey of hope and restoration

HAZEL CONWAY

Unless otherwise indicated, all Scripture quotations are taken from the New International Version © 1978 New York International Bible Society, published in the UK by Hodder & Stoughton.

MSG – The Message, Copyright © 1993, 1994, 1995, 1996, 2000, 2001, 2002 by Eugene H. Peterson

ISBN 978-1-908393-16-6
Printed in the United Kingdom

Contents

In Memory

In memory of my loving husband, Brian, and precious son, Raymond. Always loved and never forgotten.

Dedication

This book is dedicated to my sons, Colin, Shane and Brian,
and my daughter, Sheena.
You are all so special to me and so special to God.
Also to my amazing grandchildren.
You are the apple of your Granny's eye!

Acknowledgements

This book would not have been written without the help of some key individuals. I would like to thank Tim Pettingale for all his skilled editorial advice and implementation, which has facilitated the smooth and efficient publication of a book I have wanted to write for years. I also want to thank Judith Forster for the wonderful person she is.

Thanks too to my dear friends Jeannie and Bernie who have been there for me from the beginning of it all. You have seen me at my best and my worst and carried on being there for me! Thank you.

I am blessed to be in a wonderful church family, some of whom have encountered similar situations to my own. To know that we can walk our journey through life in a community that really cares is special beyond words. Thank you.

Foreword

One traumatic, life-changing phone call in a pastoral situation can leave a minister struggling for the right words in order to bring some comfort and divine explanation. Several traumatic phone calls are almost beyond belief and leave the pastoral mind questioning the very plan and nature of God! "What was God doing? Where was He going with this?" Surely those were not unreasonable questions to be asking.

If this is how I was feeling in the sequence of events that were unfolding, and are now recorded in this book, what were Hazel and her family feeling as the Lord took them into the very eye of the storm - several times?

This is the true story of a journey, often filled with fear, desperation, death, and an ongoing battle with God over His plans as they unfolded in what initially appeared to be an unjust manner. It is, however, the story of that same God, who deeply cared for Hazel and her family and lovingly surrounded them. It is about a Saviour who is still presently delivering on the promise He made never to leave or forsake the ones who will trust Him with their lives.

The Lord has been, and is, with this lovely family. He has upheld them in the darkest places and in the most devastating times. He knows what they have gone, and are going, through. He knows; He loves; He cares.

On this painful journey for the Conway family, there were many questions. There still are. There are answers - there are always answers with this God. Some have been revealed; others await His heavenly timing.

This book has not been written lightly, nor with any motive other than to honour the God who has honoured Hazel Conway with His awesome presence. To Him the glory is given. From Him the strength to live comes. With Him lie all those answers encased in perfect, faithful, divine love. I warmly challenge you to immerse yourself in its pages in the hope that you, too, if not already, will find, know and experience Hazel's Lord.

Mark A. Patterson

Introduction

I have written this book primarily as an offering to God, who has never failed to love me regardless of the times in my life when I have ignored Him, struggled with Him, used Him and doubted Him.

The New Testament parable of the prodigal son in Luke chapter 15 is a constant reminder to me of how God never stops wanting a relationship with His children even when they run away.

Life does not always go the way you think it will. If I had known when I was a child what would happen to me and my family throughout the years to come I would never have believed it.

I wanted to tell my story as a testimony to God's faithfulness and love, trusting that He will use it to encourage all that read it. I want you to meet the God I met. God is real, His love is never ending, and whilst He does not always deflect tragedy and pain from hitting us, He will hold our hand on the journey through it, even if we can't feel it, or want nothing to do with Him. He is also very patient. He has waited for me to come back to Him, weary and worn out from grief and pain, ready to heal me, and encouraging me to laugh once more.

I have waited years to write this book. It never seemed like it was the right time, despite my friends and family encouraging me to do it. I knew though, that one day the time would be right and I am glad to see it finally complete.

It is very much my own story, and I did not want to speak on behalf of any member of my family, and much of what is written is personal and subjective. Everyone interprets events and feelings differently, and this is especially true in families. I hope that my family will be gracious with any interpretations of mine that may differ from their own, and show me grace and mercy!

I want to honour every name mentioned in this book. Of course, the primary honour is given to God, my Father, King and Friend. My hope is that as I tell my story in the pages that follow, the other names that are weaved into it will be held high before God as names to honour in turn. The names of my grandparents, parents, siblings, husband, children, friends, pastors and others are imprinted in my heart as some of them are in this book, and I am deeply grateful for them all. Life is made richer by love. When we are loved we become even more lovely, and can love more fully in return. In my biased view, I am very blessed to have been loved by the best people on the planet and I pray that their lives are made richer by my love for them.

Although pain and grief can be a lonely road, it can be soothed by living in a community of people who really care for you. For me, the relationships with my family and my church family have given me the strength to walk through the darkest days. I know I have not always been easy to live with and I know that the grief will have made me self-centred at times. If you are reading this and are on that road, just keep walking, and let the people who love you minister to you. Likewise, if you are looking in to a person's life right now, not knowing how to help them in their pain, stay close, be sensitive and pray for them every day. They need you, even if it doesn't seem like it.

My hope is that you will read my story and be encouraged by it. I am not one of those self indulgent people who loves to talk about herself the whole time; I simply knew that I could no longer keep quiet about the reality of how God has treasured me when my life was both good and bad, happy and sad. His love is constant, full and deep. How could I keep quiet about that?!

Hazel Conway
November 2011

1. Early days

I was born into a farming family so have always been surrounded by fields and animals of various kinds. Mum and Dad had started their married life in Dad's family farm about three miles from Ballygawley in Co. Tyrone, later in 1963 buying their own land in order to establish a farm and family home for themselves there. It is a beautiful part of the world with rivers, streams, glens and rolling hills as far as the eye can see, and to this day I live on the same land where I spent my childhood.

There were seven children: two older brothers, Norman and Raymond and four younger siblings, Ruth, Ronald, Mary and Beth. Our lives were characteristic of a farming family in Ireland in the 1950s and 1960s, my parents working hard to make a living and keep us clothed nicely and fed well. We may not have had a lot of material things but I always felt loved and wanted. I do remember being given dolls to play with, as I would love to comb and style the hair of my younger sisters who were willing volunteers, most of the time! Looking back, I am grateful that I never really wanted for anything, for knowing I was loved has been by far the most important thing for me. I may have been a very strong willed child, frequently nagging until I got my own way and rarely taking no for an answer, but my parents were kind and loving towards me and all of their children, which built strength and value into our family unit. In the turbulent events that were to come, I see now how the firm foundation of family and church life would sustain me, even if I did not always realise it.

Life on the farm

Inevitably, as there were seven of us, there was always someone to play with, and when we were not at school or helping Mum and Dad on the farm, we would have fun making up games to keep us occupied. We certainly had plenty of space for hide and seek and we would love to be outside, whatever the weather.

There was always lots of work to be done though, and keeping a farm was hard work. Whether the cement floors needed scrubbing, the hay needed cutting and tying, or the potatoes were ready for harvesting, we all joined in to get the jobs done. One of my least favourite tasks was digging for the potatoes because I really hated getting my hands dirty and I had to scrub my hands for a long time afterwards in order to make them clean again. In direct contrast, one of the best jobs on the farm was sitting up with Daddy while the pigs were born. It felt so good to be close to Dad in a warm pig house, waiting for the tiny piglets to make their entrance into the world. Sometimes we would be there all night and I remember the feelings of anticipation watching a sow in labour, followed by the feelings of joy and relief as new life emerged.

As well as pigs, we owned a few cows and Mummy would show me how to milk them. She was obviously so much better than me than milking but I remember that I could manage to get, if not a full load, perhaps a bucketful which I would be quite proud of to be honest!

In the early days, there would be no tap water so we would carry water from the well when we needed it and as there was also no electricity, we relied on other methods of light and heat. The farm had its own bog and as a family we would go out cut the turf in the summer, laying it out to dry in the sun ready for storing to provide fuel for the winter. It was just one of those things most people did in those days, before alternative methods of heating came in. I have such fond memories of going to the bog clutching a picnic packed by Mummy for our lunch, which contained eggs that we cooked in the bog over a fire. They tasted so good!

My school was situated at the bottom of our road and I would walk there and back every day. Out of all the subjects at school, reading and English, in particular, were my least favourite. I preferred the craft lessons where we would be taught knitting, sewing and weaving. I had some lovely friends in those days, and I would often invite Pamela, Mary and Irene back to the farm to play.

All my children attended this same school, but in time it was sold to a local businessman and life long friend.

Life in the church

We were, and still are, a Christian family and from an early age I remember being taught the gospel. Both my parents went to church and so as children we would accompany them. I can't remember a time when I did not attend church and in those days it became an important feature of my life.

Knockonny Baptist Church was founded two hundred years ago and during my childhood, the building itself was small and made of tin. Today, I am still part of the same church, which is a wonderful thriving community, situated a few miles from the original tin building and built in part by my Dad in 1961.

As a child, my Sundays were full of meetings in one guise or another. There would be an hour of church and then an hour of Sunday school as well as the prayer meeting, which I would go to with Mummy. She used to pray out loud and mention us all by name in the service, which was a bit embarrassing at times, but looking back, I am now so grateful for her prayers. Mum never saw all her prayers answered in her lifetime, but I know that none of her prayers for us have been wasted and God heard every one of them.

With my sparky personality, I found it hard to keep still and quiet during the meetings and many was the time I would be told off for one thing or another and made to sit next to Dad! Apart from the fact that they were long meetings I knew that if my parents thought it was important we went, God must be real and true, and I was happy to be there, singing the hymns and letting the truths of the gospel sink in to my heart and head.

Church wasn't all about meetings though, as every year we would have great Christmas parties when Santa came, and in the summer there would be day excursions to the seaside at Port Rush which everyone thoroughly enjoyed.

My childhood understanding of God

I cannot remember a time when I was without the knowledge that I needed God in my life. From these early days, listening in church to the preachers talk about salvation, I always knew I needed a relationship with God to get to heaven.

If had done something wrong or been naughty or disobeyed (which was every day in one way or another!) I remember going to bed and standing on the landing in order to hear Mummy's voice. It was then that I knew the world hadn't ended and I was left behind to live another day. I was afraid of my loved ones going to heaven without me. I wanted to hear Mummy's voice so that I could be reassured I had another chance to go back to God and ask for forgiveness for the wrong things I had done. Over the years I have come to understand so much more about the nature of a relationship with God whose grace and mercy are freely given, but as a child I feared being eternally separated from those I loved. One of the triggers for this was undoubtedly the verse in Matthew's gospel...

'Two men will be in the field; one will be taken and the other left.' (Matthew 24:40 NIV)

...which had conjured up such a graphic image in my mind that I thought it could happen at any time and I would, because of my disobedience, be the one left alone in the field.

For a child like me strong willed and feisty, there was always a big battle between my right and wrong behaviour, and I would feel that as God only wanted obedient children, I was constantly letting Him down and disappointing Him. I seemed to always be asking for His forgiveness one way or another, rather than accepting that He loved me for who I was. Whilst I will be forever grateful for the grounding that I was given in the Christian faith, as I have journeyed through life, I have come to realize that as God made me in His image, He has always loved me and always will, warts and all! He has lovingly helped me with so much, and shaped me to be more like Him with every year that passes.

Teenage years

It wasn't until my teenage years I was properly saved. Up to that point, I had relied on the faith of my parents but as I grew older I knew I wanted to make the decision for Christ myself. I don't remember how it happened or who was there to lead me to the Lord, but I recall it being so real to me. Something had changed inside of me, and the Christian faith became clearer in my mind.

I found myself crying out in prayer for those I knew and loved who were not walking with God in a similar way, just as my Mum did before me. It was at this point that I began to understand the importance of prayer in a journey with God, which was to become more and more important in the years that followed. This verse from Philippians challenged me to live my life trusting God, submitting my fears and concerns to Him regularly in prayer.

'Do not be anxious about anything, but in every situation, by prayer and petition, with thanksgiving, present your requests to God.' (Philippians 4:6 NIV)

Baptism

I remember the day of my baptism very well. I even remember what I wore, (a swimsuit) and I have vivid memories of going under the water and coming back up again. My parents and members of my family were there to see me make this public confession of my faith in God, and I was happy that they shared in it with me. I had been well discipled in the faith, so I knew what I believed about God, what the Bible taught about God and humanity, and how I would live my life with Him. It would be untrue to say that I was a mature Christian at this stage but I knew that I wanted to follow God and baptism was a public confession of my intention.

In His grace, God covered the things I didn't understand at that time, as He does with each one of us. Some of life's most significant moments with God are the ones we understand the least, but nothing is lost to Him. If I didn't know what fully walking with God meant when I got baptized, that was less important to Him than the choice I had made. The resolve in my heart was to be committed to Him and I know that He understood me. Whatever was to come, I know that my decision to be baptized all those years ago was another part of the unshakable foundation laid in my life that stayed secure when my world fell apart some years later.

I want to encourage you that nothing is ever lost. Whatever life has dealt you, and however bad things have become, God has preserved your life and He remembers the promises you have made to Him over the years. Every prayer and every confession you have made is written in His book of your life and nothing can rub it out. It does not matter how far away you are from God, He remains always close to you. There is a lovely verse in John's gospel that has encouraged me in my times of pain as it reminds me of God's unfailing commitment to us in every season of our life,

'You did not choose me, but I chose you.' (John 15:16a NIV)

Bright lights beckon

Soon after my baptism, I joined the Baptist Youth Fellowship. As teenagers in the 1960s and early 1970s, it was inevitable that we began to find the local talent more interesting than the message. I had some strong relationships in the church youth group and we had some occasional fun together, but I was aware that I needed more. The preaching and more formal approach to social life within church was at odds with what I could see happening outside of it. I am in no way criticizing the church, or the value of good Bible based teaching for teenagers, but a healthy social diary of activities would have been good too! It was understandable, given my personality type that I would hunger for more fun and laughter within my age group, especially as I was beginning to notice boys. I wondered then how I could be both a Christian and enjoy life at the same time. It felt maybe like it was either one thing or the other, so soon the strain began to show.

I loved God and did not want to walk away from my Christian faith, but I felt I needed and wanted more than God whose image had become too serious and intense for me. I know now, of course, that God enjoys it when we are happy, as joy is part of His character and nature, but at the time, God and church were so intertwined that they merged into one. God became the church, so everything that we did reflected on what I thought God was like. I didn't realize at the time that I could take God wherever I went, as He was not confined to four walls. Church is a wonderful expression of who God is, but He is more than that too and can meet people anywhere. I remain 100% grateful for my Christian heritage but as I reflect on my life and the years that followed my baptism, I would have been helped by a better understanding about how to live for God both inside the church, and outside it.

In 1969 around the age of fifteen, I remember going to my first pub with my cousins. I was probably seen as 'the religious one' and there was some shock that on one hand I could be professing to be a Christian whilst on the other I was happy to hang out in a pub. The only thing I knew was that this new life began to offer me all the excitement I was missing. It wasn't long before I knew I needed to cross the sea to live in England where life was much more exciting.

Leaving home

I told my parents I wanted to go and live in Manchester and they were not at all keen on the idea as they felt I was much too young. Reflecting on it now, all these years later, I understand their reticence and I would say they were right, but at the time I was very persuasive, convincing them to let me stay with my cousins, Frances and Tony.

Mummy was adamant that I shouldn't go, but for Daddy it was different. He felt that if something awful happened to me in Ireland and they had stopped me going, he would have been to blame. Allowing me to go was, ironically, his way of protecting me. The first time I ever saw him cry was when I went away. He couldn't bear to say goodbye to my face, as he was going to miss me too much. This continued to be the case every time I visited them from Manchester; Daddy would never be there to wave me goodbye. I understand this so much more now as a parent myself, but at the time I had my sights set on a life away from Ireland and the promise of fun and all I wanted was my parents to be happy for me.

In truth, once I was in Manchester I missed home very much. I had flown the nest at sixteen and had to grow up very quickly in so many ways. Even though I thought I was mature, I was really still just a child. I stayed in contact with my parents, writing home every week and I cherished the letters Mummy sent me in return. People around me must have realised part of me ached for home because I remember Tony saying he didn't know why I was there, since I missed home so much. It was true. I missed the security and love that was so freely given to me back in Ireland: no one cared about me as much as my family. The promise of bright lights and fun took me away, not to a better quality of life, but to a life that offered the opportunity of living a different way, with more relaxed boundaries and fewer rules.

It took me no time at all to make friends. I soon met Bridget who had been a neighbour of ours in Ireland and who had come over to Manchester at a similar time to me. We became firm friends, going regularly out together on the town. It was through Bridget that I met Brian, the man who was later to become my husband.

After years of helping my parents on our family farm, I discovered that I wasn't lazy or afraid of hard work. I knew I needed to take more control of my life in Manchester, as there was no one there to pick up the pieces if it all went wrong, so I made sure I was never without a job. I worked as a waitress in shops, hotels and cafes, often on my feet for long hours, but the advantages, especially in waitressing, were that the tips were good, often better than the wages themselves. Being chatty and friendly, I had a good rapport with my customers, which built my confidence that I was able to take care of myself. I was growing up, but in a different way from how I would have done had I stayed in Ireland. There I would have gone to church more, but for the duration of my time in Manchester, the only time I set foot in a church was the day I was married.

Interestingly, though, I did take my Bible to Manchester with me and my cousin Tony would often encourage me to read it, I think to honour my Mum's wishes. I am grateful that he at least tried to keep me on the straight and narrow, even though living as a Christian was becoming less and less important compared to a life of drinking and late nights.

Imagining who I would have been had I not gone to Manchester is difficult because in hindsight, I probably had to move away from the familiarity of home to realise who I really was deep down. I had started on the road to where I am today. Also, had I not moved out of home all those years ago, I would not have met Brian or had my five children who have blessed me so much. I would have lived as a more traditionally religious person and that would have hindered me from understanding my own children when they began to push their own boundaries growing up. The snap decision to go to Manchester was to shape my life so differently and lead me out of a sheltered existence. Life in church is good for the reason that it does shield us from so many temptations, but while I wouldn't suggest anyone lives my life the way I did, in reality, I know I am a rounder person now with God's help, than I would have ever been had I not made the decision to go.

In addition, it has given me a greater love and compassion for those young ones who feel the same pull of alcohol and other things. It is so easy to criticize them, but so much better to pray for them without judgement and with grace, and I find it easier to do that given my own history.

God is gracious to us. He understands when we mess up and feel like we have failed. If you read this story of my life and have more revelation of God's grace, then I will be more than happy! The Bible tells us we have all fallen short.

'For all have sinned and fall short of the glory of God.' (Romans 3:23 NIV)

But whether we are harsh in our judgements, making immoral choices or drinking heavily, God is always full of grace. It is a real relationship of love, not a set of rules and God looks first on the heart, not on the behaviour.

'But the LORD said to Samuel, "Do not consider his appearance or his height, for I have rejected him. The LORD does not look at the things people look at. People look at the outward appearance, but the LORD looks at the heart."' (1 Samuel 16:7 NIV)

Throughout all this time in Manchester, when I was drinking regularly and living a life far from the framework I had been taught and in which I had grown up, God held me even though I couldn't feel him and even though I didn't want Him. The prayers of my loved ones, particularly my Mum, as she cried out to God for us all by name day after day, were invaluable for us all.

Now, as a Mum and Granny myself, I realise how vital those prayers were, and am so grateful for them. I pray in the same way for my own family now that my Mum did for us all so many years ago. God has answered so many of my prayers I have prayed and continue to pray for my loved ones, because He hears every one and is faithful to answer.

I am here today as testimony to the prayers of others so I want to encourage you to commit to a life of prayer. It is not hard and the rewards are great. Never stop talking to God about things, even if circumstances in your life or the lives of those around you look like they will never change. God is always there and can change things to reveal more of His glory, as we shall see in the chapters ahead.

Our kids' school photo

2. Independence and early married life

'"For I know the plans I have for you," declares the Lord, "plans to prosper you and not to harm you, plans to give you hope and a future."' (Jeremiah 29:11 NIV)

This Bible verse is very special to me. Many times as I look back over my life, I can testify to the goodness of God, even when I didn't feel His presence. Life is a mix of highs and lows, twists and turns but God never changes, and His promise in this verse remains as true today as it has always been.

If someone told me when I was a child how my life was to pan out, I would never have believed it. Had I known some of the things that would happen to me and my family I would have hidden away; but I didn't know what was in my future, and I couldn't see anything ahead. I had to walk through life, day-by-day, step by step, some days holding on by a very thin thread to a God who I hoped knew how to help me through it. The wonderful thing is that not only did God know about my life, He was, and is, committed to prospering me, protecting me, giving me hope, and assuring my future. I pray that this verse is as encouraging to you as it is to me, whatever you are facing in your life at this time.

Meeting Brian

Life in Manchester continued in a whirl of working by day and socialising by night. I was getting used to my independence and enjoyed the freedom to mostly come and go as I wished. Living with Tony and Frances offered me security, and they were very good to me in those days. I missed home, but my new life offered me far more excitement than I would have had back in Ireland, so I wasn't prepared to give it up just yet.

After about a year, I met Brian Conway, an Irishman from Derry. The first time I saw him I was in my friend Bridget's flat in Manchester and I remember thinking that he had the most fantastic eyes I had ever seen. Brian was three years older than me but he was years ahead of me in maturity. Even though I was trying to be physically and emotionally all grown up and independent, I still needed protecting, and something about Brian felt safe, secure and steadfast, even on the day of our first meeting.

When it was time for me to go home from Bridget's that first evening, I nonchalantly asked the group of people there who would walk me home and that they were not all to jump at once! It was Brian who led me home that night which sparked the beginning of our friendship.

Over the next days, we became closer and I used to chat happily about home, telling him about my family and the farm. It was lovely to spend time building a new friendship and quite soon, Brian and I became an item.

Marriage

I was still drinking and was intent on having a good time most nights after I finished work. Life had quickly settled into a pattern, and I expected my relationship with Brian would just be a part of my wider social scene.

Brian was a Catholic and as I wasn't, but despite all of our disagreements and occasional childish behaviours, we decided to get married. I remember how we wrote to both sets of parents together and posted the letters on the same day, informing them of our intention to wed.

The wedding would be held in Manchester and the logistics of who would marry us and where, were understandably complex. With our different expressions of faith, we had to reach some sort of compromise somewhere. We also had our families to consider and neither of us wanted to hurt them or dishonour our respective heritages. In the end I agreed to the marriage being held in the Catholic Chapel with a blessing in the Protestant Church of Ireland. As a response to our wedding taking place in the chapel, Brian agreed that any children we would have together in the future would be taken to Sunday school with me.

We were married on the 25th November 1973. From Brian's family, only Brian's sister Maureen attended the wedding as she lived in Coventry at the time, which was less of a distance to travel. My Mum, aunt and brother Raymond (who gave me away) came over from Ireland and I was so glad to see them.

Even though we were getting married in church, God was not an important part of my life. To be honest, I was too consumed by my new relationship with Brian and the thrills of life in Manchester to think about being religious. I felt I had lost my faith, and considered myself unsaved, so being 'unequally yoked' as Catholic and Protestant did not really matter in the grander scheme of things. I felt that as I was not walking with God, why should it matter?

I was still in my teens and as the saying goes, you can't put an old head on young shoulders. The wedding day was happy, yes, but I couldn't help feeling that life was rushing away with me and I wondered what my future would hold. Brian, being the more serious one in our relationship, had not married lightly at all: he had married for life and that was that.

Children and responsibilities

Inevitably, children soon came along and our first son Colin was born when we lived in our little flat in Manchester. We were overjoyed to be parents and so proud of this little life that had been entrusted to us. I remember bringing Colin home from the hospital and feeling that no other child could be loved more than we loved our son. I wanted to shout if from the rooftops how wonderful it all was.

I adjusted quickly to motherhood and Brian similarly got used to being a Dad with no problem at all. He was at his happiest being with the children and me, and he made sure we wanted for nothing.

It was about this time that I began to learn to pray. Every night I would pray that my son and any other children we would have, would grow up to love and serve God. I didn't feel awkward talking to God, probably because I had grown up in an environment where praying was a normal part of life. Like every child, I absorbed what was going on around me in my family without realising it and so my prayers just came out naturally.

Colin was loved so much. My previous yearnings to go out socializing gradually began to fade away as I focussed solely on being a wife and mother. Our relationship grew stronger and stronger. This handsome man with his blue eyes, dark hair with grey streaks, strong hands and big heart, was so good for me and so good to me. I wasn't always easy to live with, but his gentleness would never fail to win me over. He was the best man I could have ever hoped for, even though I didn't always realise it. It is so easy to overlook the gifts of love in other people. We focus on the negatives without stopping to give thanks for the positive qualities in those people God has given to us in order that our lives will be blessed. We do not always know what we have until it is gone from us, so why not take time today to be thankful for those who love you, as Paul says in the Bible,

'I thank my God every time I remember you.' (Philippians 1:3)

We bought our first house in Manchester a little two up two down and were mortgaged to the hilt. It needed a lot of work doing to it, so Brian used his skills as a joiner and handyman to make it into a cosy home. There was nothing he couldn't do and he worked so hard. We may have had very little money to our names, but they were such happy days. Our personalities complimented each other very well: Brian a man of few words, and me perhaps a little more vocal, for instance!

Our second child Shane was born in 1975 and it was at about that time I really began to miss Ireland and my family there. I wanted to go home. Brian loved living in Manchester but as was usually the way, I managed to persuade him that it would be good for us all to move back to Ireland and establish a new family home there, renting out our house in Manchester in case it didn't work out.

At this time, the conflict in Northern Ireland was in full flow, and the hunger strikes were dominating the news. I never felt scared by this, or concerned about how my relationship with Brian would be viewed, mainly because as children we were brought up to respect other people's beliefs. My parents encouraged us to celebrate relationships and respect all people, for which I have always been very grateful. I remember my Daddy once hiding a Union Jack we had in our house, in order to save offending our lovely neighbours, Tommy and Alice Goodfellow. They were family friends of ours for as long as I could remember and despite all the conflict going on around us, my parents were determined to preserve the friendship at all costs, never encouraging partisanship.

As we lived in a rural area we experienced very little of the conflict over the years, although of course we would see news reports on the television. Helicopters would occasionally land nearby, dropping off soldiers for exercise, and driving our car into a sensitive area would require a police search, but in reality, it was inconvenient more than dangerous.

With the arrival of Shane, Brain and I knew we could love another child as much as the first. When I was pregnant, we had wondered how we could share our love equally, but we needn't have worried! Shane was a delight to us and with the other three coming along in succession, Raymond in 1976, Sheena in 1978 and Brian in 1981, our family was complete and we knew such happiness together. Each of my children are loved the same and that will never change.

In the process of building a family we also created a home on Daddy's land. Brian spent three years building it, mainly after finishing his long days at work. I still live there to this day, grateful for the care and skill Brian employed in making his family such a beautiful home surrounded by the hills and valleys I grew up in.

Where I was with God

My faith had been buried underneath all the stuff of life and I felt that to some degree I wasn't really worthy to be called a Christian, as I was not living in an active relationship with God. Having said that, nothing was going to stop me praying for each of my children to embrace the faith that I believed was right, but was no longer active in my own life.

Brian would go to Mass every now and then and I would drop the children off to Sunday school at Knockonny Baptist Church. Even though Brian had promised me that the children could do this, it didn't mean he found it easy to watch them go. I remain deeply grateful to him for such a sacrifice. As the years went by, he even agreed to take them to their Sunday school on the way to Mass, collecting them on his way home. This was a big thing for him and I want to honour him for it. I did not return to church myself for quite some time, as I knew I was not ready to wholeheartedly commit myself to it. I wanted our children to be raised in the same faith I had been taught, but I knew I was not at that point, alive to God myself.

I have thought about this a lot over the years. I can see how God has answered the prayers I have prayed for my children, as they are all saved and are wonderful examples to my grandchildren. I may not have been the most diligent in accompanying my children to church when they were children, but God is their Father and will lead them Himself. Where I fell short, He covered it, as He understood my heart's desire for them. Not only does God know the plans for your and my future but He has plans for our children too. Be encouraged that He takes our best efforts, hears all our prayers and nothing is ever ignored. If you are concerned about your children's salvation, keep praying for it and do as the Bible says,

'Cast all your anxiety on Him because He cares for you.' (1 Peter 5:7)

Mummy

I was seven months pregnant with our third child, Raymond,

when we were told that my Mum had cancer. It was a Saturday night and we had gone to the hospital with her, as she had been unwell. The nurse came in and asked Dad to go and talk to the healthcare professionals. I was left sitting with Mummy, Brian and my sister Ruth. Daddy never came back and when visiting time was over Mum kept asking why Dad wasn't back, so I reassured her that he probably had been given good news. In truth, the opposite was true. My Mum was never told she had cancer, but multiple sclerosis, which may seem like an odd thing to do these days, but years ago, no one talked about cancer and the patient would certainly not have been told if they didn't need to know. It would be the next of kin that heard the truth. For me, it was the first time I had encountered cancer or even serious illness and I didn't know how I was going to cope watching Mummy get sicker and sicker.

Eventually, she came home from hospital, and my sister Ruth gave up her job to look after her. When Raymond was born a few weeks later, Mummy and Brian came to the hospital, so she was there just after he was born, which I was so glad about.

Mum lived for thirteen months after the cancer diagnosis. The first few months had not been too bad but she suffered a great deal towards the end. During the time she was ill, and after Raymond was born, our family went back to England for a few months to sell our house. I think Brian knew deep down that with Mum so sick, we couldn't go back to living in Manchester, as the family would all need to pull together.

My youngest sisters, Mary and Beth were only ten and eleven at the time, and they especially would need tender loving care when Mummy had gone. Ruth became the primary carer but between us, we became the support my younger sisters needed.

The day Mummy died, I watched Daddy, Mary and Beth together. I remember talking to Mary a few years ago and remarking on how awful it must all have been for her and Beth, but she told me she remembers so little of the rawness of the grief because Ruth especially did such a good job of caring for them. No one told me how to comfort those who were in grief, but even though I had my own loss, I am thankful I was able to reach out and help my sisters in a small way.

This was my first encounter with grief and Brian was very supportive and kind throughout, even though I didn't always see it. He was just always there for me, mostly quiet and behind the scenes but always strong and always reliable. Everyone grieves differently and Brian understood that I needed time to work through losing my Mum in my own way. He knew that the day I received the diagnosis about Mum was as bad if not worse than the day she died, and he just walked with me through it all.

Learning to adjust

Our family has always been very close. In those days, Brian would remark on the kindness and love that runs like a thread between each of us, one to the other. When a parent dies, everyone in the family has to adjust to a new position and that takes time.

We didn't hurry it, and gave Daddy in particular the space to grieve his own way. As was the way with that generation, he would not talk about his pain, but expressed it in different ways.

One of the things he could no longer do was to live in the home he had shared with Mummy so he built another home next door to Brian's and my house in which he still lives to this day. Brian had always felt very loved by Mummy and Daddy who had welcomed him into our family with open arms.

Throughout this time, I continued to pray for my children's salvation without compromise, even though I was still picking and choosing how and when I would live out my own Christian walk. I knew that praying for them day by day was the right thing to do, and how glad I am today that my prayers for their salvation have been answered.

However, within myself, I held an ever-increasing anger towards God. I don't know where it came from or why it was there, but in the future I would see evidence of it as I went through my own personal sorrows. Perhaps I had never been really close to God, so when I was faced with circumstances that were painful or that I didn't understand, I would get angry. All I know now, though, is that within it all, I would come to a place of truth as I recognised that even though I had strayed far away from the God who loved me, He had never left my side.

Raymond

3. Raymond

As I write about the events that follow, I am aware that this is a very personal account of my family's experience with tragedy, which will never of course be identical to any other family's journey through loss. I have written it as honestly and openly as possible, not to indulge in my own story, but to offer encouragement to the reader. The account may be mine in detail, but the emotions in it are universal: shock, pain and grief are experienced by us all at some point in our lives and as I write about my son Raymond, my prayer is that God will give you comfort and hope that no matter how bleak life can get, He is faithful to His word.

'The Lord himself goes before you and will be with you; He will never leave you nor forsake you. Do not be afraid; do not be discouraged.' (Deuteronomy 31:8 NIV)

With the house in Manchester now sold, Brian and I could focus on planting our family roots back in my hometown in Ireland. Everything felt different without Mummy and I missed her terribly, but we all pulled together and gave as much support to Daddy as we possibly could.

Life went on with the usual ups and downs. Over the next few years with the arrival of Raymond, Sheena and Brian, things became busier and busier. Like all young mums, I became completely focused on raising the family and creating a stable home, coupled with a day job in a chip van.

Life was very good and there was always so much happening one way or another. At home, the kettle was always on, as I happily made endless pots of tea for the people who would drop by to say hello. As they grew up, the children would have friends to stay, and the house was constantly full of noise and chatter.

As a skilled joiner, Brian had started a kitchen business called Conway Kitchens, which was based in a workshop next door to our home. He worked very long hours in those early days in order to get the company off the ground so to provide a good standard of living for us all. Today, Colin carries the main responsibility for the company and I see so much of Brian in him. Colin possesses a stability and strength, wit and gentleness that make him not just a great craftsman, but a wonderful son, husband to Cherry and father of three children, Grace, Hannah and Jude, all of which would have made his own father very proud indeed.

Raymond   41

Everything changes

There is a saying that we do not know what we have got until it's gone, and I would say that is certainly true. Looking back on my life prior to 1994, I did not know how blessed I had been up to that point. As a family, we were about to be tested to the limits of endurance by loss so deep I thought we would never recover.

Sheena

In March 1994, at the age of sixteen, our daughter Sheena was crossing a road near where she worked as a shop assistant in a filling station, and was knocked down by a car. Brian and I received a telephone call from her boss while we were at home, and we rushed to be by her side. It was a phone call that every parent dreads, and during the minutes we drove to the scene of the accident, we tried not to imagine the worst. Arriving to see quite a few people standing around, we realised the paramedics were fitting her with a neck brace. As our only daughter, Sheena was, and still is of course, very precious and loved, and to see this happening to her broke our hearts. As well as being a hard worker, Sheena is a fantastic mother to Nicole, Aaron and Jamie, and loving wife to Nigel.

She was to be taken to the hospital and even though I was not sure whether everything would be all right with her, Sheena kept reassuring me she would be fine. I was allowed to travel in the ambulance with her, still wearing my slippers from home, and Brian would drive our car behind us. I had been told by the medics that she was likely to have no serious injuries so I was feeling calmer, but I thought about Brian following us, not yet aware of this news and still therefore in a highly anxious state. I remember wanting to reassure him somehow as the drive for him must have been so lonely, but I had to trust that God would comfort him where I could not.

Once we were at the hospital, the neck brace was taken off, revealing no major damage, for which we were so thankful. Sheena had bruised her back as she hit the ground, which had caused some swelling so she needed to walk on crutches for a while, but that was the only injury she sustained. We brought her home two days later and were able to go on our much-anticipated three-week holiday to France after all.

The event had shaken us all. I remember Raymond telling me later that he had been in the workshop when we quickly left to see Sheena at the scene, and a deliveryman had dropped something off, saying that there had been a bad accident where a girl had been 'thrown in the air like a rag doll.' Raymond had instinctively known the man was talking about his sister, and had had to live through the next few hours, not knowing whether she was severely injured or worse.

At this time, Brian had been struggling with the loss of his own father who had passed away three weeks earlier. I remember as we came home at the end of that long day of the accident, he announced that there would be no more fighting in our home, and that we should all go to church. He told me that while he was driving the car to the hospital following the ambulance, he had made his peace with God.

The desperation I had felt at not being able to reassure him that Sheena was unlikely to have sustained serious injury as we drove to the hospital had been completely covered by God. Brian had had his own conversation with the Lord that day, coming to a place of peace and rest within himself, drawing great comfort from it.

God is so good! He lifts the burden of our anxiety from our shoulders and answers our prayers for our loved ones. When, for some reason, we are unable to be there to support and encourage each another, He does it for us.

If you are feeling burdened about someone and frustrated that you can't be with them, perhaps now is the right time to release it all to God, remembering Jesus' words as he promised:

'Come to me, all you who are weary and burdened, and I will give you rest. Take my yoke upon you and learn from me, for I am gentle and humble in heart, and you will find rest for your souls.' (Matthew 11:28-29 NIV)

Raymond

It was the 26th September 1994; a normal Monday morning like any other. In those days, I owned a big saucepan in which I used to cook potatoes, and that day I wanted to use it to cook the dinner for the evening. I hunted high and low for it, only to find that Raymond had taken it to wash his car. As was always the way, Raymond had shown his more resourceful side in borrowing my pan for the car wash, and I remember thinking I could not even be cross with him for doing it.

Raymond was like that! He was a real character: fun loving, witty and cheeky but with such an affectionate disposition.

Taller than the other two boys, he loved tinkering around with anything mechanical, anything that had an engine in it. Out of all of the children he was also the one who loved animals the most, and being brought up on a farm was to prove a brilliant thing for him as he enjoyed being alongside the livestock.

He was dyslexic and many a time would struggle with school, frustrated that he found reading so challenging compared to his peers. What he lacked in some areas, he made up for in others, namely his cheekiness. His teacher would tell me she would often have to turn her back on him as his mischievous antics would make them laugh too much, when really, she was required to be stern with him for playing up. It was at about five o' clock that day, while I was on the yard retrieving this potato pan, when the police car drew up. The policemen got out of the car, not wearing their helmets, asking me if I was Hazel Conway. When I replied that I was, they requested that we went into the house as they had something they needed to tell me. I refused, knowing that if, as I suspected, they came bearing bad news, I would not be allowed outside again in order to run away.

So, outside in our front yard, the police this time quietly asked me if I was Raymond's Mum. I answered that I was and they told me he had had an accident at work. From that moment, I would not let them use any more specific words to elaborate on what had happened, as I knew deep down that whatever had happened was fatal and that Raymond was dead.

I must have screamed. I remember Brian coming out of the workshop, probably wondering what kind of mischief the boys had got up to that merited a visit from the police. Colin and Shane followed close behind, and together we stood on the green circle of grass at the front of our house listening to the police talk. Shane had already heard on the radio that a young man had been killed at work that day, and as I looked over at him standing there, I knew he knew it was Raymond. I will never forget his face at that moment. He had his hands to his head, crying, 'Not Raymond, not Raymond!'

Shane and Raymond were especially close, always hanging about together and messing around as lads do. Out of all of the four sons, Shane was, and probably still is, the most like Brian physically. With his soft heart and kind ways he has, over the years, become a family man of the best sort who loves his children Shay, Kacey and Jayden so deeply, and his relationship with his wife Tracey reminds me so much of my own relationship with Brian.

Our lives are shattered

Our whole world collapsed that day; there is no other way I can describe it. In an instant, everything had changed as we experienced the irreparable tearing apart of our family unit.

Much of what happened in the minutes that followed remains a haze even to this day, but I do remember running down into Daddy's house, opening his front door and shouting 'Raymond's dead.' I wanted to run and run, far away from it all, desperate not to face the truth of what had happened, but I knew I could run nowhere. I had to face it head on.

In some ways, this was a reflection of the truth that grief is something we cannot run away from even if we want to. The journey is best walked through the middle, not around the edges in denial, or running in the other direction. I would learn this in the months and years to come but at this point, I had no idea how I was going to cope with any of it.

We remained in the yard for what seemed like a very long time. There was nothing anyone could do. The police asked us if we wanted them to tell anyone about Raymond's accident and as our son Brian was at my sister Ruth's house at the time, Shane went with the police to tell them the news. Sheena was brought back home from work, still recovering herself from her accident just a few weeks previously. She had seen the ambulance and fire brigade driving past while she was there, and knew something serious was unfolding.

Eventually, we all filtered back into the house and Brian and I came in the living room, hugging each other again and again. The pain was etched onto the faces of Brian and the four children and as I looked at each one of them I experienced even more sorrow.

Raymond's accident had happened at work between two and three o'clock that afternoon, and all I know is that it involved a forklift truck. I do not know how he actually died, I did not want to know any details of what actually happened and the same is true to this day. For some people, it is imperative they find our every detail of an event like this, sifting through the information to help them in their grief. I am not like that at all. No one way of grieving is more right than the other, so we need to leave people room to process their loss in the way that is best for them, not putting pressure on them either way.

It was only during the process of writing this book that I have been able to visit the site where Raymond died seventeen years ago, and I am glad to have done this now. My children had already been there some time ago, but until now I have never wanted to see it. I realise that my journey into full healing continues, step-by-step, year-by-year as I progress through life with God by my side.

On the day we heard about Raymond, everyone I loved came to our house to be with us. I remember how my friend Ann came to cook and clean for us, and as I write this, how she is now encountering the same pain through the loss of her own son. My other friend Jeannie also came that day, unable to comprehend the truth of what had happened, as we all were. Life had been normal when we woke up that morning, and in one brief moment, it would never be normal again.

All of a sudden, too, we were public property, as a report of the accident appeared in the local paper. This made me very unhappy at the time, as we had not given our consent to it. I felt it exposed us as a family at a time when we needed to grieve privately. If I had had the strength, I would have sought to stop this happening. I simply preferred that the whole community did not have a window into our personal lives at such a raw time.

The morgue
After he died on the Monday, Raymond was taken to the

morgue and we had to go and see him on the same day, which was an hours drive away. This is another thing I bitterly regret happening in those days. Whilst I know all the reasons why it was necessary, it added a great deal to our pain, as I just wanted to bring Raymond home. I feel quite strongly that no one should ever have to go to a morgue if it is not wanted. Seeing Raymond there, in an unfamiliar room felt so exposing when all I wanted to do was grieve for him in private, at home. For us as a family, it served no benefit or purpose, and it is one of those things I have needed to reconcile over the years. Again, everyone copes with loss differently and my struggle may not be the same as others, but I wanted to include this because I think it is an important issue. Sometimes we just need courage to override the norms of protocol to preserve what we believe is right for us and our families.

Raymond comes home

For the three days after Raymond died we were immersed in the funeral arrangements. I found it hard to focus on anything at all as my emotions were all over the place: it felt like I was in a thick fog. I kept remembering how Raymond had come in to our bedroom on that Monday morning to say goodbye to us before setting off for work, not realising it was to be the last time we would ever see him and talk to him. The doctor came and did offer us tablets to dull the pain, but said that in the end, it would be better for us if we faced the grief head on and walked together through it. In hindsight, it was very good advice.

The wake

It is traditional in Ireland to have a wake where the body of the loved one is brought home in order for people to come and pay their respects. For two days, friends and family bring food and occupy the home to share in the loss and to some extent, help soothe the shock. On the day of the accident, people came to get the house ready to receive Raymond's coffin and I remember being grateful on one hand, but angry on the other as they wanted to take down stickers and posters from the walls in Raymond's bedroom.

I know they meant well, but in my grief, I wanted everything kept the way it was: changing it made Raymond's death more real. In the end, as Brian did not want Raymond lain in his own bedroom, the coffin was placed in our bedroom. I remember the lid was leaning against our wardrobe door and to see the dates and the name, 'Raymond Conway', so clearly written on it was truly horrible.

I spent a lot of time with Raymond when he was brought home, going in and out of our bedroom to see him. I would talk to him too, watching him intently so that I would always remember his face. I never wanted to forget his face.

There was a constant flow of people coming through the house during the wake. So many, from young to old, wanted to pay their respects and support us in our pain and loss. Grown men would come out crying. I wonder how people can walk through grief without the love of a community around them and I sometimes reflect on the erosion of family and society in our world and feel sad that there is so much loneliness and isolation. Our local community and church family were vital to us then and for me now, they still are.

It was during the wake and in the middle of the night that I called out to God. I didn't share this with anyone for a long time, except maybe my pastor, Mark, as it was an intensely private thing for me. I knew that if I was going to make it through and be of any use to my family I couldn't do it in my own strength. I needed God to help me do it. I don't know what I said, but I do remember expressing my dependence on His presence to carry me through whatever was to come. I did not feel anything, but I knew He had heard my cry and that had to be enough for me. I could not feel warm towards God because I was so angry at the loss of my son, but I knew I needed Him, as this journey was too big and complex to walk without Him.

The funeral

Raymond was buried on the Wednesday. Family members who made sure we were included in every important decision that needed to be made organised the funeral. Brian and I were so grateful to them and for them. There was no way that we would have had the presence of mind to plan it ourselves. Pastor Mark Patterson was in our home throughout those days as were the elders and members of the church. We were so appreciative of their prayers, support and offerings of love in so many guises.

As the children had been brought up in Sunday school at Knockonny Baptist Church, it made sense for Mark to conduct the funeral and for Raymond to be buried in the graveyard there. He preached a gospel message at the service itself, and so many people were hurting to see our family struggling at the loss of our son and brother. I think that if people could have taken our pain away there and then, they would have done.

Since we had received the news about Raymond, I had never wanted to leave Brian's side, I needed to hold him and be close to him, but as he and the children were carrying Raymond's coffin I was forced to let him go. Pastor Mark took my hand and as sure as I held Mark's hand I felt God take my other hand and we walked the hill together. God's hand felt very real and this was the first time I realised how close His presence was to me. I needed it to get through the day, but it is only years later that I came to understand the preciousness of the moment that day.

I appreciate so much all that was done for us as a family over that time, even though I was then preoccupied with my own grief and could say very little in the form of thanks. Lovely food was prepared for after the service and I remember picking up something tasty, and trying to eat it but it got caught in my throat, as I was unable to swallow food. I know my friends and family understood my lack of obvious gratitude at the time, but now, all these years later I want to use this opportunity to thank them all for their loving care. We couldn't have done it without you, and I am so grateful to God for giving us such a loving community in which we share our lives.

'How good and pleasant it is when God's people live together in unity!' (Psalm 133:1 NIV)

4. Learning to live with loss

Everything had changed. In the days after Raymond's accident, I knew that life for me and my family would never be the same again. How could my life continue as it was when Raymond's had been so suddenly cut short? I knew I had responsibilities to my husband and my other four children, but part of me had died along with my son, and I did not know how I could live my life without the presence of Raymond in it.

I had all of a sudden begun to hate and fear the dark, so Brian installed lights outside our home to keep everything as bright as possible. Perhaps this is one of the characteristics of grief that as daylight fades and activity stops, the sadness can be overwhelming and sleep is elusive. I knew I needed sleep so the lights were left on all night to push away the bleakness of the night.

Of course, Raymond was always on my mind. I carried him with me constantly and not one minute went by in those days when he was not with me. He was my last thought as I went to sleep and my first thought as I awoke. Sleep went some way to restoring my body, and both Brian and I were grateful for it, but did nothing for the emotional turmoil that had enveloped us.

With each passing day, Raymond's death became more real to me. Initially, when the news of the accident reached us we were all in shock, and to some extent everything seemed like we were living in the middle of a very bad dream. However, after the wake and the funeral, we were faced with the days, months and years ahead of living without Raymond.

Although friends and family continued to call on us for many months afterwards, it was after the funeral that the six of us had to come back to the house as it was. The furniture needed to go back the way it had been, looking like it did when Raymond was here with us. A few days earlier, he had lived with us and now he never would again. He would never sit in the chairs, sleep in his bed, eat at the table or lark about in the garden.

I prayed and prayed in those days that God would send him back to us, but of course it didn't happen. I was beginning to understand that this was only the start of the journey of walking through the stages of grief ahead of me. I wanted Raymond back so desperately and for everything to go back to how it was. I remember thinking about the days before the accident, wishing I would have stopped to reflect on how blessed I was to have a wonderful family around me, thanking God for my husband and five children, but it was now too late.

The television sat silent in the corner of our living room. I had no idea what was going on in the outside world, and had no desire to know. I was all consumed with my own pain and I had no room in my heart to care about anything else. Where the children would have sat and watched their favourite programmes together, they were now lost in their own worlds as they tried to come to terms with the loss of their brother. My eldest boy Colin had loved football and used to kick a ball around the garden at every opportunity. It broke my heart to now see him walk past and ignore the ball in front of him as if it wasn't there.

I understand now how grief reshaped us all differently in those days. As a family, we had shared the same experience but because we were all different, we all needed room to mourn differently. One person's grief is different from another, and if you are reading this at a time of loss, know that your journey through it is unique to you and you need space to walk it your way, just as your loved ones need their space to do the same. I want to encourage you to be real and honest about where you are at so that God can lead you into peace on the deepest level.

For example, Brian took particular comfort from the sympathy cards that were sent to us when Raymond died. The words contained within them meant a great deal to him and helped him feel closer to the memory of his son. However, in contrast, when we would visit the grave in the days after the accident, Brian would look at the mass of flowers and wreaths placed there and struggle with the riot of colour they displayed. He found them gaudy in his world of grey. He would say that our lives were empty and colourless and this grave, so full of colour, was not an accurate representation of how we were living. It wasn't that he was ungrateful for the flowers people had lain there as expressions of love and sympathy, simply that they did not help him in his grief.

At home, I struggled to cook food for the family. Before Raymond had died, making meals was a part of my role as wife and mother and I enjoyed being in the kitchen. But I quickly came to hate it, for the simple reason that I always cooked too much. I think that deep down, I was continuing to cater for Raymond, and throwing the leftovers away just brought back to me that he was no longer there. This was nothing to do with not wanting to care for my other four children; rather that it was one of the aspects of grief that I encountered as I struggled to let him go. Sitting at the table and eating together, especially on a Sunday, was a reminder to all of us that there was an empty place that would never be filled again.

Back to work

For some time before his death, Raymond had joined Brian in the workshop, and for Brian to even consider going back there was very difficult, despite being one of those men who were just made to work. But life marches on relentlessly and there were bills to be paid, so about two weeks after the accident, and with some gentle persuasion from a neighbour, Brian went back to the workshop followed soon after by Colin and Shane. With hindsight, I think this was very good for them because it gave them a focus, and whilst nothing about our situation had changed and Raymond was never coming back, the routine soothed them. It also meant that any financial pressures that could have added to our strain were averted, for which I was grateful. It is easy to feel guilty for 'getting back to normal' as if somehow it is not honouring to the life of the person who has passed away, but in my experience, that Brian and the boys returned to work was an important part of looking forward, as well as looking back to remember Raymond's own role there.

My days

I found that as the days went by, I needed to fill my time differently. The house was so changed and I found it very difficult to adjust to it. Sheena and young Brian had gone back to school leaving me to my own thoughts, which were with Raymond all the time. I did continue to cook and clean but my priorities had inevitably changed.

Some people need time alone to grieve but I found I didn't need my own space. In fact, it didn't seem to matter whether I was with people or not, I just tried to get through each day regardless of what was going on around me.

I couldn't eat anything in those days; all I could do was drink water or tea. My sister used to come every day and bring mushrooms, which for some reason were the only thing I could keep down.

I existed in a vacuum. At one point I went to the doctor, as I was concerned that all I could do was smoke cigarettes, eat mushrooms and drink water and tea. He replied that whilst it wasn't advisable to be on such a scant diet with cigarettes, it would do me no harm in the short term. I was glad of the advice as it took the pressure off me needing to change. Grief is exhausting and all consuming, and trying to manage a balanced diet and give up smoking would have been something I could not have done without a momentous struggle. I was thankful my doctor recognised this and advised I focus on other things.

We had changed our sleeping arrangements, as Brian could not bear to go into our bedroom. Raymond's coffin had been put there for the wake, and for Brian, the memories were too raw for it to be a place of rest. So together, we slept in Raymond's bedroom for a long time, sharing his bed.

Anger with God

Around this time, I was very angry with God for allowing Raymond to die. Pastor Mark would visit and listen to me rant and rave, unable to contain my rage both at the series of events and the lack of answers to my questions. I struggled with a God who the Bible told me was all loving, but who seemed to be punishing me for turning my back on Him all those years ago.

Again and again I would ask Him why He had done this, only to receive no reply. I was desperate to make sense of Raymond's death. Mark was so patient with me, always listening, never making me feel small or silly as I struggled to come to terms with what had happened. I will always be grateful for that.

I watched my family hurting, and saw the pain in their eyes. Nobody knew how to handle the emotion, and there were many tears in those days. Brian had never really cried up to that point, but now it was often that I saw him break down.

One of the aspects of grief is that it changes people who you thought you knew and whilst at the time it was difficult, I know

now that you have to let people express new emotions in new ways and not expect them to conform to how they were before.

I know I needed God but I didn't want Him. I needed His strength to live through what had happened, but in my anger, I found that my relationship was built on what I needed to get through, not what I could do for Him. At times, I felt God had me trapped against a wall, and I could only slip away from Him in the mornings, when it was light and I felt able to cope. By the time the night came, I would need Him again and would tell Him everything. It was a seesaw relationship, which was full of honesty and emotion. I could not fake it, and looking back, I would never have been able to pretend that I could rejoice in everything because I couldn't.

It's good to be real with God. In Matthew's Gospel, Jesus says,

'Blessed are those who mourn for they shall be comforted.' (Matthew 5:4 NIV)

Mourning is not always pretty, not always quiet, and never nice, but God has promised in the Bible that He will bless those who are going through loss. This is as true for you if you find yourself in that place as you read this book, just as it has been for me.

Keeping things the same

Raymond's room stayed the same, as it always had been when he had lived. His clothes hung in the wardrobe and his favourite posters remained stuck to the walls. I would not let anything be moved. Nothing was touched. Eventually I would be able to let Raymond's things be moved, but I knew that in my grief I needed to treasure his things as part of him. There is no right or wrong way of doing this, but it is important not to rush ourselves to clear things away before we are ready.

Counselling?

I had days when my emotional elastic band was stretched to breaking point. Every day it would come into play at some stage and there was one day when I walked the fields with my aunt not knowing whether I would see the day end.

Looking back we probably could have done with both individual and family counselling. It is often with hindsight that we would do things differently and this is one of those things I would have changed. All that we were going through in being forced to let go of Raymond was new to every one of us and none of us knew that grief could be so bad as emotions bounced all over the place. Even though my Mum's death was so awful, I remember talking with my sister Ruth and asking if we ever really grieved her as it felt so different with Raymond. We did, of course, but it highlights how every loss is different.

These days, counselling is more readily available for situations like ours and it is a good thing to consider if you or your family need it. But I have to trust that God has covered my family despite all my thoughts on this, and He has been their strength.

Learning to be honest with God

My relationship with God was secondary to my grief over Raymond. As I have said previously, He was there because I needed Him. I needed Him for me alone and I couldn't begin to think about telling anyone else about Him or share with anyone about His love. I want to be honest about this because it is important. I am not inviting anyone to disrespect or dishonour God, rather, to be honest with Him. When things didn't make sense in the days and weeks after Raymond's death I needed a God on whom I could 'pour out my soul' (Psalm 42:4). Based on my background and upbringing, it is not something I thought I would ever say but a real relationship with God has room in it for honesty. How could I pretend that my life was OK when it wasn't? I chose not to walk away from God but to face Him and tell Him the ache in my soul and my struggles with my unanswered questions. From where I was, God was not making everything OK and I remember thinking that I was stuck in a life without Raymond and I needed to be honest about how that made me feel.

Grief is all consuming and unbearable, and my own experience bears witness to the fact that at times, it left no space or capacity in my heart to be kind about God at all. I was fighting for survival and God wasn't bringing Raymond back to me. I won through in the end but nobody could have told me I would come through it at the time. It was just day-by-day. Someone once came to me to tell me how God gives and takes away which to be honest, I found quite unhelpful. There are times when platitudes don't work. Sometimes a handshake is better than a preach!

My cousin once left a little book for me with very simple words in it, which I found became a real comfort, as I couldn't read much. It explained how God can handle our emotions and how it is not always helpful to quote Bible verses to someone who is grieving, because words can feel like a burden if the person is not in a place to receive them. I understand that. People do mean well but it is impossible to convince someone out of their grief. All the head knowledge we may have about God doesn't stand up to our experience at the times when the rawness of life kicks in and you are tested to the point of nearly dying yourself.

I remember thinking no one loved her son more than I loved Raymond and no one hurt as much as I hurt. No one's grief was ever as bad as my grief was. No one knew what this was like and no one could pretend to know.

Pastor Mark continued to have the patience of a saint and he understood that I needed to walk through my journey of grief and not be rushed. I think he knew I would come through it with God! He was always there when I needed him the most and I have a fond memory of the day I was making something to eat while I was weeping, only to see that he was tearful too.

Out and about

I still needed to go to the shops for food. I would see Raymond's favourite Pot Noodles sitting on the shelf and waves of sadness would wash over me as I remembered how he would look forward to eating one on a Saturday night. Going to the school reminded me how Raymond was glad to leave it, because he didn't like going there at all.

The National Lottery had launched at the time of Raymond's death and everyone was talking excitedly about the prize money. I remember thinking then that even if I had done the lotto and won it, it would not have made my life any easier because I had a hole in my heart that nothing could fill.

Everything was difficult in those days.

I started going back to church a couple of Sundays after Raymond died and even though I cried most Sundays, I took an enormous amount of comfort from being there. The children came with me, which I knew was hard for them, as teenagers tend to hate tears at the best of times, but I felt it was important they were in church with me. I would sit in the back seat so as not to draw attention to myself and more often than not, I was the last into the building and first out.

I am so grateful for the prayers that were prayed for us all in those days. If I hadn't have been in a church I know I would not have benefitted from the results of those prayers that helped me so much. Looking back, I know that God definitely answered them. It is very important that we pray for one another and never underestimate the power of your prayers for those who are suffering loss: they are vital!

Christmastime

The first Christmas after Raymond died in 1994 I went to buy family presents with my sister-in-law Nora, but I hated the carols and the shops glowing with lights on the trees. It felt like people should not be celebrating when I was in so much pain. Every year I had always bought the kids selection boxes and I remember that year picking up five of them, bringing them home and telling Brian who said, 'Don't worry about that, the fifth one will be mine.'

These may sound like insignificant memories, but for someone grieving they were huge. It is often in the seemingly small things that the loss is the most acute and the loneliness can take our breath away.

I have never sent a Christmas card since Raymond's death but I do have a Christmas tree now. The year before Sheena left to get married ten years ago, we got a tree and it was very special for us all. There were times in the early days I could not have done that, but as the years go by, and with God's help, there is healing.

For Christmas in 1995, Brian and I bought Shane a ticket to the darts semi-final in Sheffield so the three of us plus Brian's brother Terence went there via London for a few days. It was lovely to arrive in London knowing that nobody knew me, or our situation. I felt I left a burden lift off me as I left Ireland for that time and I became almost normal in my anonymity. It was just what we all needed and something I can highly recommend if you find yourself in a similar situation we were in.

Grief upon grief

In 1996 Norman, the eldest of my siblings, died in a very short space of time. He had been born partially sighted and as a boy, had been to a special school for the blind in Belfast. He was diagnosed with schizophrenia and was in and out of hospital quite a bit over the years. Norman could be very gentle in his clearer moments, but the schizophrenia sadly changed him to the point where at times, that gentleness was undetectable. He died very suddenly from a tumour no one knew he had. I thank God he didn't have a protracted death, since to watch him suffer would have been terrible. Once again, Pastor Mark was on hand to help us through our sorrow, always praying for us and believing in the goodness of God to heal us.

On the day Norman died, so many people came to our home as they had two years before, parking their cars in our drive as well as Daddy's. Brain had been out fitting a kitchen and when he came back to see so many cars, he was overcome with emotion, thinking it was another of his children who had died. I remember he hadn't the strength to get out of the van that day. All the memories had flooded back to him of when Raymond passed away. It was terrible for him, and even today, I can remember seeing the pain and fear in his face and eyes. At the same time, our neighbour's son had a serious car accident and died in hospital the next day. We attended two more funerals so close together; two more lives wiped out in such a short space of time.

We were overshadowed by grief but Brian and I became closer and closer as a couple. Our lives felt like they had ended when Raymond died, and then we faced the grief again with my brother's death we realised life is very precious, so we decided to make the best of trying to live again. We began to go out more once going to see a show in Dublin, which was a lovely day. This was the first time I had heard Brian sing in the car for two years. I remember touching his hand and feeling overwhelmed by love and thankfulness for such a precious husband and life partner.

Our wedding day

Me & Brian - a day in the countryside

Brian singing country music

5. Brian

'Trust in the LORD with all your heart and lean not on your own understanding, in all your ways submit to Him and He will make your paths straight.' (Proverbs 3:5-6 NIV)

If we could understand everything that happens in the course of life, then there would be no need for this Bible verse above. The simple truth is that there are times when we need to lean into God because there is simply nothing else we can do when life makes no sense. When we are at the limits of our understanding, the Bible calls us to trust in God and not try and work things out ourselves, because once we try to do that, we get confused and everything is a mess. I am not saying it is easy to trust God, and I am not saying I always get it right even today, but I can tell you that I have learned to live by the truth of these verses and I know He makes my 'paths straight' when I choose to trust Him for my life.

More loss

I had already had to accept the fact that Raymond was never coming back which had tested me to the limits of my understanding, and beyond. Now I was about to face another sudden loss and once again I would have to choose to trust God in the shock, pain and confusion as my world fell apart once more.

On the 23rd December 1996, at the age of forty-five, my husband Brian died.

It was a Sunday, two days before Christmas day. Although nothing was, and ever would be, the same again after Raymond's death, our family would be together over this period and I took some comfort from that. We all missed Raymond so much but two years on from the accident, we were learning to walk again, even if it often felt more like we limped together.

That frosty evening, I came home from church to find some of the family sitting around with Brian having a cup of tea, and we chatted together about how he had built our home with his own hands. He seemed very happy and relaxed: everything was completely normal and there was absolutely no hint at all of what was to come. Eventually, people went home and I decided to go to bed around eleven. Brian wanted to watch a music programme on the television so I left him to it, looking back as I left the room to give him the thumbs up as he sat in the corner of the room and he responded with a smile.

I fell asleep but awoke an hour or so later to find that Brian was not in the bed beside me. I got up and went into the living room only to see him lying on the floor, so I rushed over to him only to hear him say that he had bad pains in his chest. For some time, Brian had suffered with severe indigestion, which would give him terrible pain. I initially thought that this was the cause this time, but as I watched him, it soon became very clear to me that the reason for this pain was altogether different. I asked Brian if the pain was worse than the indigestion and he told me that it was, so I rushed into the kitchen and made up some soluble painkillers as quickly as I could in order to ease his discomfort.

While I was doing that, I resolved to make a doctor's appointment after Christmas to see what could be done for Brian, as I couldn't bear to see him in this state. I never thought at that point that it was anything serious or life-threatening, simply because I believed that I had had my share of shock and sorrow and God would never again let anything like that happen to me as long as I lived. I believed that my life would continue into old age, with my husband by my side, a journey of learning to live without Raymond and watching our family grow around us. How wrong I was.

Brian drank the soluble tablet with my help, and I waited for it to take effect, praying it would happen quickly. All of a sudden his eyes rolled back in his head and I made a snap decision to ring for an ambulance. I think I just went into automatic mode, unable to grasp the implications of what was happening, or analyse what the end result could be. It's like my mind could cope with certain things but not others and the overriding element was to stop Brain's pain.

It seemed like we waited a long time for the paramedics to arrive, during which I rang some others to see if they would come to be with us. Our friends Pat and Bernie, Daphne and Eamonn, who had been at our house earlier, and who all live locally came up straight away. I remember Pat went looking for the ambulance, because as time passed and Brian continued as he was, we all began to see that it was a very serious situation and Brian was fighting for his life.

By this time, the children, who were still all living at home, had woken to the noise of the commotion in the living room. Colin and Shane took one look at their Dad and knew that he needed mouth to mouth resuscitation so that's what they did; one of them massaging his heart and the other breathing oxygen into him to help him stay alive. I was still in the kitchen on the phone to the emergency services who were helping the boys by relaying all the information they needed to know.

Our son, Brian stood in the hallway as the go between, repeating what I heard the medics tell me to Colin and Shane. In some ways everything was going in slow motion and in other ways it was frantic as we all fought for Brian. We were bang in the middle of a terrifying situation that had crashed into us from nowhere, but I felt in some ways like I was in a daze and it was happening to someone else. None of us had any choice but to live through the events unfolding before us, holding on to the hope that Brian would live.

But Brian lost his life that night. He died on the living room floor in the house he had built, with his children all around him. The ambulance arrived, but the paramedics could do nothing for him, as he had had a massive heart attack from which he could never have recovered.

There was so much sorrow. My children were all crying and I remember my heart aching deeply for them all as I watched them try to come to terms with the loss of their Dad. After all the frantic and noisy activity around the attempts to save Brian, the house was now quiet except for the sound of weeping. I knew at that moment that ahead of us lay another journey through grief, with all its associations, and we would have to learn to live our lives without Brian. He had been our rock, our provider, and our protector. He was a wonderful father to his children and a treasure to me. Not one of us could imagine life without the presence of Brian in it.

All this time I had stayed in the kitchen, and I had absolutely no desire to go into the living room to see Brian at all. I wanted to remember him smiling at me as I went to bed that night, not lying lifeless on the floor. I had telephoned Pastor Mark who came as quickly as he could for which I was grateful, and later the priest came too. I remember going outside through the back door to walk around in the sharp cold, often barefoot in my pyjamas, with Pastor Mark and my sister Ruth keeping an eye on me wherever I went. I didn't care about myself, or my appearance, I just wanted it all to be a bad dream from which I would soon wake up and life would return to how it had been.

Meanwhile, the paramedics needed to get a doctor to the house in order to pronounce Brian dead. Even then I still could not go in to the living room, though everyone else did. I am not sure exactly why this was but I do remember struggling with the truth of what had happened. I was not sure that I was able to face reality at that time, and perhaps I was in denial. I did not want Brian's death to be true, and by staying in the kitchen I was maybe creating a little distance between truth and unreality so that things could change if at all possible.

I write this to convey the complexity of shock, which can render people unable to function normally. It was my love for Brian that kept me in the kitchen. I wanted him to be alive, not dead, and to see him that way was something I would have been unable to bear. Remember to be kind to yourself and others if ever you or your loved ones go through something like this, and leave room to process the shock in the ways you or they find most natural.

As it was now Christmas Eve, we had some decisions to make about the funeral. I decided that because we knew from the medics that Brian had suffered a huge heart attack there was no need for a post mortem. And since I was against any of my loved ones being taken to the morgue after my experience with Raymond, the funeral was to be held on Christmas Day.

Everyone was watching each other as we tried to handle the shock of what had just happened. We hugged and wept together, sometimes speaking, sometimes lost in our own thoughts, always wondering why this had happened and how we would live through the loss of Brian.

He was so loved by so many! This man had such kindness and grace; was a hard worker, committed husband, father, son, brother, uncle and friend. How could he possibly have left us so quickly? And how would we live without him? It was terrible. I am not clear on the exact timing of this but at some point over those hours after Brian died, the realisation hit me that I was now solely responsible for the home, the business and the welfare of my children. I knew I would need to step up to the mark and would have to make some important decisions in the weeks and months ahead and I doubted at that moment whether I was remotely capable of doing any of it.

The comfort of God

Now, all these years later and with the benefit of hindsight, I can write freely about the goodness of God, and how He offered me help time and time again when I needed it the most. It was like He gave me the resources to handle things I never thought I could. I learned quickly that he is close to widows as it says in the Bible:

'Your widows, too, can depend on Me.' (Jeremiah 49:11 NIV)

If you are reading this and you are widowed, I want you to be encouraged because God will not let you go under. He draws especially close to those who have been abandoned, for whatever reason and whatever the circumstances, giving comfort, help and peace when we need it the most. I look back over the years since I lost Brian in amazement at what I have been able to achieve with His help and you will too when you trust Him to lead you through.

At the time of Brian's death, I struggled to make sense of why God would do this to me again. When Raymond died, I was not walking closely with Him and to some extent it brought me back to my faith, but this time I was actively living the Christian life and I thought that I was now immune to such tragedy.

The truth is of course, I wasn't and none of us are. Tragedies happen all the time, both to those who are saved and those who are not, but the key thing to remember is that God will provide all that we need to live life in all its fullness.

He knows our angers, our pains, sorrows, bitterness and grief, just as He knows our joys, celebrations and successes. The Bible tells us that Jesus was acquainted with grief and that God gives comfort when we mourn.

'You who are my Comforter in sorrow, my heart is faint within me.' (Jeremiah 8:18 NIV)

Two years previously, part of me had died with Raymond and now I felt that Brian, who was the other half of me, had taken that half with him to his grave. I had raged at the death of my son, and God knew it all even though I was not walking with Him at the time, but when Brian died, I found the same rage was not there. This grief was different: no less raw, but different. I was beginning to experience God's comfort in a new way.

Between the deaths of Raymond and Brian there had been a change in me. I had found a peace in the storm of the loss of my son that really did surpass my understanding. I somehow knew that I could trust God to lead me through this second devastating loss as He has done with the last one. I remember Pastor Mark used to encourage me to see the bigger picture of things. It wasn't always what I wanted to hear if I felt consumed by my own pain, but eventually I realised his words had sunk into my soul. When Brian died, I had a peace that God just knew the bigger picture. I could now lean into Him when things didn't make sense and I struggled to understand why I was a widow in my early forties.

Losing a child is, in my view, as bad as a pain can get. Children should outlive their parents and the loss of them strikes at the core of the human heart.

When Brian died, I was still grieving the loss of Raymond, and to some extent my brother Norman, and I was not sure how I would be able to cope with any more pain. Brian and I were married for twenty-four years and we had become closer through the death of Raymond.

In the quiet moments after Brian died, I remembered how he held me after Raymond's accident, his own heart breaking, hearing him tell me how he could always make things better for me, but how this time he was unable to. Of course he couldn't, but we helped each other and now he had gone. I really was being thrown onto the love and mercy of God and we would get through it together.

Brian is laid to rest

Brian's body was brought back home on Christmas Eve and I looked at him for the first time since he had died. Memories of Raymond flooded back as Brian's coffin was brought into the home and placed gently in the same place in our bedroom that another had laid two years before.

I looked at Brian's face. I wanted to imprint the shape of it into my memory so that I would never forget it. This face had smiled, frowned, wept, laughed and very occasionally, shown anger. Now as he rested in his final hours at home with us, he looked so peaceful. I touched his face, and wept over a life cut short.

Brian's mum and three brothers Terence, Gerry and Seamus came that day and his sister Maureen who lived in Coventry came a little later. That day the house was full of people coming to pay their respects, and I realised afresh at that time just how loved Brian was. People came from across the community to honour him and stand with us as a family. I will never forget it.

Over the weeks prior to Brian's heart attack I had bought and wrapped all of the family's Christmas presents ready for Christmas morning. I had shown Brian what I had bought for each of the children so it seemed right to carry those presents into the room where Brian lay, placing them at the bottom of the bed beside his coffin as an acknowledgement that this would be his last ever Christmas with his family. It was a comfort to me, as I hope it was to the children, and one of those spontaneous and tender acts of love that can stand out as lights in the darkest times of loss.

The funeral was held on Christmas morning. Brian was first taken to the Catholic Chapel, led by the priest at the time, Father MacVeigh who was very good. After the service, Brian was to be buried beside our son Raymond, and my cousin Tony sang this song in the chapel:

I Know Who Holds the Future

I do not know what lies ahead,
the way I cannot see,
But one stands near to be my guide,
He'll show the way to me.
I know who holds the future
And He'll guide me with his hand
With God things don't just happen,
everything by Him is planned.
So as I face tomorrow,
with its problems large and small,
I'll trust the God of miracles,
give to Him my all.

I do not know how many days
of life are mine to spend;
But One who knows and cares for me
will keep me to the end.
I do not know the course ahead,
what joys and griefs are there.
But One stands near who fully knows,
I'll trust His loving care.
(Written by A.B. Smith and E. Clark)

Following the service we travelled to Knockonny Baptist Church
for the burial and had a graveside service held by Pastor Mark.
Both the chapel and the church were packed with people
who knew and loved Brian, even though it was Christmas Day.
Everyone wanted to be there.

At the church, I watched as my four children, Colin, Shane, Sheena and Brian carried their father's coffin to the graveside where he would be buried beside their brother. I had decided not to have food at the church in order to allow people to get back to their family Christmases, even though Pastor Mark had offered it for which I was very grateful.

Coming home

So when it was all over, we went home to begin life without Brian. I felt very weak with the emotion and the anxiety about the future, and was carrying a deep concern about the way forward for each of my children. They had encountered such loss in their young lives and I did not want any more of it to overwhelm them ever again. To this day, I pray for them all and for their own children that God would answer my prayers for lifelong health and safety for each one of them and that my grandchildren will never know the pain of such grief.

I was changing during this time.

I was utterly devastated at the death of Brian and wondered if I would ever feel whole again, but unlike the grief of Raymond I had allowed God into my life in particular ways that meant I was able to process my emotions more with Him than without Him. This didn't mean that I went around in a holy bubble! Far from it! I was still honest with God about the unfairness and pain of Brian's premature death, and would never pretend that life was good because it wasn't. It was simply that over the last two years, I had begun to meet God in a new way and deep down I knew my need of Him and my desire to walk ever closer to Him in the years ahead. I had encountered His grace working in me and very carefully I was beginning to trust Him in a new way and trust in this grace to see me through.

'My grace is sufficient for you, for My power is made perfect in weakness.' (2 Corinthians 12:9 NIV)

6. Life without Brian

A short time after Brian died, it dawned on me that I was about to face the biggest challenge of my life: learning to live without my husband. I could almost feel the weight of responsibility on my shoulders getting heavier by the day. All of a sudden I was in the position of having to be both mother and father to four children who were all still living at home at the time, even though the oldest two were adults.

It was not just the practicalities of feeding them, clothing them and paying the bills, it was how I was going to be able to provide for their emotional welfare and well-being. They needed me to be strong. We had all lost Brian and each of us would be affected by that in our different ways, but I was the Mum, and I could not shirk my commitment and responsibility to the needs of my children.

When I looked into their four faces and saw their grief, I realised I had two stark choices before me: either I could give up or I could try to live again. I chose the latter. I had cried for two years since Raymond died, and I knew I could do this no longer. In fact, I wondered whether it was physically possible to weep any more tears for that long ever again.

The children had seen me cry for all that time and I did not want them to have to go through it all again. Also, I found that was changing too, and whilst I would never want to convey that the grief over Brian was any less real, I had begun to encounter the comfort of God in a new way. I could feel my relationship with Him deepening through the pain.

'Do you not know? Have you not heard? The Lord is the everlasting God, the Creator of the ends of the earth. He will not grow tired or weary, and His understanding no one can fathom. He gives strength to the weary and increases the power of the weak. Even youths grow tired and weary, and young men stumble and fall; but those who hope in the Lord will renew their strength. They will soar on wings like eagles; they will run and not grow weary, they will walk and not be faint.' (Isaiah 40:28-31 NIV)

I no longer wanted our home to be full of tears, and I imagined a day when it would be full of joy and peace. We would grieve Brian of course, but I did not want people walking into the house and feel nothing but anger and pain. Neither did I want friends to stay away from the home because of the heaviness in the atmosphere. When he had lived, Brian was such a contented and peaceful man who loved his home and family and I knew that it would have been the last thing he would have wanted if the home he had built was filled with misery.

The home

My home has always been very important to me. I am not the type of person who has to have the very best of everything and my home has never been full of expensive trinkets or designer furniture. But it is the place where I feel the most rested.

Walking into each room today, I can recall the memories of the years of family life at its best and at its worst, the laughter and tears, noise and peace, stress and calm and I am deeply thankful to Brian for building this home so lovingly for us all. It still stands as a legacy to him, not in a bleak or mawkish way, but a proud testament to his commitment to us as provider and protector.

The house was built on top of a hill and although the wind certainly buffets it at times it remains as solid as a rock year on year. I love living here, whatever the season, and when autumn turns to winter, the roaring fire keeps me cosy and warm.

The events of life can buffet us and threaten to tear us apart, but in God, we can shelter for protection from the storm. He has built walls around us to keep us safe so that no harm will come to us. God never leaves us unprotected, and sitting here today in the home I still live in all these years later, I am so grateful for it.

'Whoever dwells in the shelter of the Most High will rest in the shadow of the Almighty.' (Psalm 91:1 NIV)

The challenges

Colin and Shane were used to Brian being the boss of the kitchen business he had built from scratch when we moved back to Ireland from Manchester in the mid 1970s. Both boys were now skilled enough to earn a living but they would have to quickly learn about how to negotiate their way around the complexities of all the aspects of the business with which they were unfamiliar.

In the early days after Brian's death, I was fearful that I would not be able to financially support my children and that I would not be able to keep the home or the workshop. The kitchens we made in those days were made of pitch pine as Brian specialized in this area. Although they are less in vogue now, this particular style of kitchen was very popular in those days and we had a good source of timber in England and Scotland. So there would be no shortage of materials if we chose to keep the workshop going. In the end, I knew it had to be my decision so I prayed about it a great deal. I wanted to know God's will for us and I was looking for His peace, whichever path we eventually took.

I remember praying about it one day, handing over the whole thing to God, asking Him to take control. It might sound flippant or unwise, but in reality I was desperate for Him to take the pressure off me.

It was becoming a burden made all the more heavy by my anxieties and fears about the money side of things and how we would make ends meet. I had to decide the future of my husband's business, which he had loved. The two boys knew more about that side of things as they had both apprenticed with their father, but I could not let them make the decision about it's future as it would have been an unfair pressure on them.

That said, I knew that Colin in particular would have to make his own choice as to whether he wanted to continue in the workshop or not. To some degree there was an expectation on him, to continue the family's name in business, but I didn't take that lightly, nor did I take it for granted.

In the end, we decided to keep the workshop going and today it is where Colin works full time as a skilled and diligent craftsman. Shane has built his own fireplace business nearby and they are both very much involved in each other's lives. I am blessed by them both (as I am by all my children) and am grateful to Colin for shouldering much of the responsibility then and now. So Conway Kitchens was to become our main source of income.

When a partner passes away, the one left behind is required to step into the places left vacant by the death. For some, the pressure of this responsibility is overwhelming and it is easy to panic or become very stressed. My experience has shown me that once I accepted the position in which I found myself, I let go of the expectation that I needed to be perfect, or always get everything right, and I concentrated on taking everything to God in prayer.

I am not saying it was always easy, and neither am I saying I was always reasonable or peaceful but I did notice a difference when I brought God into the equation.

It is not just the partner who feels it, but the children do too. All of a sudden, Colin and Shane had to make decisions about their futures that had both pros and cons: no decision would be perfect and no decision would be without cost. They were required to take responsibility for things with no guarantee that they had made the best move for their futures at all.

We do not always see the bigger picture, but as I have mentioned previously, Pastor Mark always used to encourage me that God does. The choices we make today, often through an emotional fog where we cannot see clearly, when committed to God, will come right in the end. We have a strength we do not know is there until we are forced by our circumstances to take responsibility for our lives and the lives of our loved ones. Take courage! You may want to hide away and hope everything will disappear, but it is not likely to. Putting our trust in God to help us through is the only thing we can do.

'Those who know your name trust in you, for you, LORD, have never forsaken those who seek you.' (Psalm 9:10 NIV)

Loneliness

It dawned on me after Brian had died that I needed to rewrite my will. I remember this process well, as it brought home to me how in my life as it was now there was really no one behind me to be my mainstay and protector. I was all the children had in the role of parent, and I needed to work very hard to keep on top of everything. Even though prior to Brian's heart attack, I had looked after the family finances, Brian would not know if a bill was paid or not and he was always my backstop when I needed him.

I missed him so much! Not just in this area but every area. I missed our times of sharing and catching up with one another at the end of the day. I missed the familiarity of his ways and the way we were just so comfortable in each other's company. I had no one to talk to about the children and their lives or about our respective families.

After he died, I remember allowing myself three weeks to live. I honestly thought I could not go on any longer than three weeks without him. I just thought I would fizzle away once I had done all of the practical organisation of what needed to be done. Effectively, I imagined I would die of a broken heart as Brian had taken half of me with him that December night.

God with me

'The widow who is really in need and left all alone puts her hope in God.' (1 Timothy 5:5 NIV)

I had a good relationship with God at this time as during the night of Brian's funeral I had awoken from a broken heart, only to experience a heavenly peace come upon me soon after. As the verse here says, I was a widow who was putting all her hope in God. I felt alone, and yet in the middle of this storm it felt like my heart was outside my body and God's peace was simply overwhelming me.

I love these words of Jesus in the Gospel of John,

'I have told you these things, so that in me you may have peace. In this world you will have trouble. But take heart! I have overcome the world.' (John 16:33 NIV)

This was my experience! I had had so much trouble but I trusted the One who had paid the price for my freedom to give me the peace He knew I needed so much.

I knew God was real, even in the darkest moments. The anger that had raged inside me after Raymond died had all but disappeared, and I now wanted to take Him at His word, trusting Him with my life. I still did not know why Brian had died, or Raymond for that matter, and I wished their deaths could have been avoided, but I was now becoming dependent on the One I had fought for so long, and it felt good. This is the paradox of faith: in the middle of the storm, when everything is raging, God makes a way to still the storm and whispers peace into the heart, drawing us into His love as it says in Hosea.

'I led them with cords of human kindness, with ties of love. To them I was like one who lifts a little child to the cheek, and I bent down to feed them.' (Hosea 11:4 NIV)

In the early days, it was easier not to read from the Bible itself but to read from my daily notes or other leaflets that I was given or had around the house. I had to be realistic about my walk with God and there was no way that I wanted to pretend I was ready to spend time soaking in His word because I simply was not ready to do that yet.

What was important was that I was reading Scripture in whatever context I found the easiest. If you are feeling under pressure to absorb more of the Bible than you can, don't worry, just take smaller chunks in any way you find the easiest. God will speak to you in the ways you can hear Him the most clearly. Remember, He wants to speak to you more than you want Him to! He will find a way through your wilderness as He has promised.

'See, I am doing a new thing! Now it springs up; do you not perceive it? I am making a way in the wilderness and streams in the wasteland.' (Isaiah 43:19 NIV)

The family pulls together

So our journey of living without Brian had begun. School had started back, and although young Brian was nearly at the age when he could leave it, he struggled with going back. He missed his Dad, as all the children did, and so I decided to let him stay at home more than perhaps was best for him. As the youngest child I probably let him get away with more than the others would have been able to at that age, and looking back it was not the wisest decision I have ever made.

I wanted to believe it was good for Brian to stay at home and grieve when it may have been better for him to be with his peers. It is just an example of the dilemmas I faced being effectively a single parent, day by day. I wanted to do my best for everyone at a time when I didn't really know what the best was!

Colin and Shane were in the workshop every day and worked very hard to keep our heads above water financially. We still managed to go on holidays, which sometimes helped alleviate our loss, but not always. I wonder if the holidays were a way of escaping from reality and speeding up the pace of life so that I would heal more quickly. I wanted to get through the sorrow into a place of freedom, and filling my time with different activities and trips offered me that option I suppose. I went to America ten months after Brian died to fulfil a dream he had always had of going there, but I realised while I was there that however lovely it was, I was living his dream and not my own. We can never live someone else's dream and no holiday will ever speed up the healing process. It needs to be done at a steady pace, with God's help and the support of friends and family.

I was desperate to avoid the depths of despair I had experienced when Raymond had died, as the pain was so acute, I did not know if I would ever recover. Also, it was my first encounter with the enormity of loss, and the intensity of my emotions nearly washed me away. In some ways, Raymond's death had prepared me for the loss of Brian. Losing my husband so suddenly was no less of a grief, but I understood the journey a little better the second time around.

The stages of grief

The experts seem to agree that there are as many as seven stages to grief and I will summarise them here in the hope that you will recognise the pattern in yourself or those you are helping through loss.

The first stage is shock and denial when everything is numb and it is impossible to come to terms with what has happened.

The second is pain and guilt when everything is in chaos and life is never the same again as the realisation of the loss strikes at the heart and soul.

Third comes the anger when we look for someone or something to blame and all the bottled up emotions spill out. This is when we can say and do things we regret, and when we need good friends to stick with us most of all.

The fourth is a time of reflection and loneliness when the emptiness hits.

The fifth is called 'the upward turn' when we feel things shifting and life feels brighter albeit only a little.

The sixth and seventh stages are about reconstruction and hope as we accept what has happened and learn to live looking forward rather than looking back.

I have been through each of these stages, and most people who have grieved the loss of a loved one will have done the same.

No stage should be rushed; we need to heal at our own pace.

The wedding ring

I cannot remember exactly when, but at some point after Brian's death I stopped wearing my wedding ring. I did this because I could not bear to be asked any questions about what my husband did.

Neither did I want to talk about being a widow. Not only was it a conversation stopper, but also I did not like making myself vulnerable to people I only knew in passing or not at all. Inevitably, if people discovered I had children, they would ask how many, and I never knew whether to tell them I had four or five as both answers were difficult for me.

I wanted to avoid being pitied at all costs and by not wearing my ring, I was more likely to be considered a divorcee or unmarried, both of which, oddly, were preferable to being a widow. This bothers me much less now, which I am sure is obvious as I am writing a book about it, but in those early days, it did matter a great deal.

I believe that God made us for marriage. I understand that some people don't want to be married, feel called to singleness, or never find the right person but this does not change the fact that God once said,

'It is not good for the man to be alone.' (Genesis 2:18 NIV)

Life was made for two. I have come to complete peace on this now, but Brian's death changed everything. My identity is in God but it was also in being the other half of Brian and nothing can replace the wonderful memories we shared together. He gave me five wonderful children and I am thankful for each one of them. In addition, I have the best grandchildren in the world (I'm biased of course!) so God has always been, and continues to be very good to me in bad times and good.

'You, Lord, are forgiving and good, abounding in love to all who call to you.' (Psalm 86:5 NIV)

7. Smiling again

I am now content and at peace. I have come to rest in the truth of who God is, and He is now at the centre of my life. I know that even when I let Him down, which I often do, I can go to Him in prayer asking for His forgiveness, joy and grace to fill me. There were times when I thought I would never feel alive again but God has kept me, loved me, protected me and held me throughout my whole life and that will never change.

He is the same yesterday, today and forever and has enough love for every man, woman and child on this planet. What He has done for me, He will do for you, in whatever circumstances you are facing. God will not rush us, or demand anything of us: He waits for us to be ready to reach out to Him and when we do, He is always ready to love, comfort, heal and bless. Why not reach out to Him today?

'Shout for joy, you heavens; rejoice, you earth; burst into song, you mountains! For the LORD comforts his people and will have compassion on his afflicted ones.' (Isaiah 49:13 NIV)

Family life

I love being with my four children, their children and husbands and wives. I currently have nine beautiful grandchildren, and at the time of writing there is another one on the way so there is never any shortage of fun around the place!

Like many people, I have had many titles over the course of my life: I have been a daughter, mother, sister and aunt. When my oldest grandchild Nicole was born eight years ago, the new title 'Granny' was bestowed on me! I love to be called 'Granny Hazel' and sometimes I tell Nicole that she was the one that started it all off! Of course the little ones think I am old because I am their granny, but I never feel old and can keep up with the best of them: long may that last!

The great thing about having grandchildren is that I don't have to worry about being the one who has to supply their food and clothes, or be the one in charge of discipline and boundaries. I can just love them, indulge them, hug them and pray for them to my heart's content and have the privilege of watching them grow up in the ways of the Lord. Few things are better than that.

It is lovely spending time with them all and my favourite days are when we are all together for dinner, or having a birthday party, or celebrating some special occasion. Each time we gather as a family I am full of joy at the precious times we share.

What is most important?

Relationships matter so much more than material things. Preserving the unity, love and peace within family and friendships should be one of our highest goals and I know it pleases God when we do. When I look back on my early days as a mother, I recall my bad temper and how I was quick to show anger if, for example, something was broken. Now, as God has wonderfully taken away my anger in His gentle, quiet way, I am so chilled that if the grandkids mistakenly break something at home I let it pass me by without a word!

Circumstances have changed me, yes, but it is God who has changed me for the better. Not all who live through traumatic life events come through it a better person, as grief and loss can actually make someone more angry and bitter than they had been previously. But give your life to God and He will reshape you His way, so that you become more like Him. This is my testimony of His goodness and I am so glad I know Him.

'His divine power has given us everything we need for a godly life through our knowledge of Him who called us by His own glory and goodness.' (2 Peter 1:3 NIV)

Looking back over my life, my happiest times have not involved material things but have all centred around relationships. When my five children were small we had very little money, but the joy I experienced was to see them all growing up learning for themselves about life and love. A generation later, I watch my grandchildren doing the same and know that my children feel the same way.

Money offers a certain security and can alleviate pressure and strain but is never going to feed the deep down hunger we all have to be in relationship with God and others. In addition, material things will never, ever, replace the sadness of losing someone you love because only God can heal that deeply.

If you are reading this and you have a good life, similar to mine now, I would ask you to stop and be thankful for what you have got, not what you have not. So much time can be wasted striving to fill the need for satisfaction, when satisfaction is right in front of us in the form of our friends and families who love us, and a God who loves us so much He sent Jesus to bring us freedom.

Young Brian

In 2001, about five years after my husband Brian died, I faced one more serious trauma when my son Brian became very ill. It wasn't visible at first but I knew he wasn't well and when he told me some of the symptoms I knew he needed to see the doctor. In fact he saw a lot of doctors some of whom told us that he was seriously ill but it was difficult to be given a diagnosis without more tests.

After the first series of appointments, Brian and I would return home very heavy hearted and unable to articulate what we were feeling to each other. The doctors were beginning to mention the words 'Crohn's disease' and 'ulcerative colitis' and these were conditions with which we were both unfamiliar. All I wanted to know was whether Brian was going to die. I could not face the prospect of losing another child and the anxiety and stress at that time before he was properly diagnosed was overwhelming. Our own GP had assured Brian that what he had was not life threatening but it took me a while to come to terms with this new challenge in our lives. Brian had given the doctors permission to inform me of everything, for which I was grateful as it helped me stay close to him and relieved the fear of the unknown to some degree.

Brian endured many tests over a couple of years before the doctors decided to operate on him. He had lost a lot of weight and was very ill but he never lost his courage and optimism, or his hard work ethic over that time, which meant he continued in his job throughout, saving up to buy himself a car in the process! Brian never complained or wallowed in self pity, even when things became almost unbearable for him and all his energy was directed to just getting through each day. By nature, Brian is a comedian with a very big heart full of affection.

So in February 2004 he was admitted to hospital, staying there for six weeks while he had exploratory operations and tests. He went in as a fairly healthy looking boy but during his stay there deteriorated to the point where he became almost a shadow. When the final diagnosis came in, we were told that the condition Brian has was likely to be ulcerative colitis and although we all hated seeing him suffer so much, it was a relief to finally know what we were dealing with.

If I could have, I would have taken every last bit of suffering away from my son. Brian would tell me not to cry, but the emotions ran so deep that I found it hard to push them down. Six weeks before his operation, Brian had met Oonagh who worked with my daughter Sheena. Oonagh was, and is, an amazing support to Brian, always there for him whatever he was facing. It shows how much Brian was affected by his condition that when he was in the hospital, he refused even to see her. Initially he had the patients laughing at his jokes on the open ward, but within days he just wanted to hide under his blanket.

Eventually we brought Brian home and between us, Oonagh and all our family helped him in his recovery. We leant on each other as we cared for Brian, and shared together the pain of seeing someone we love suffer so much. In fact the whole family were suffering for him.

I wonder if the focus on Brian's condition helped me in my grief. In some ways, it halted the journey, but in other ways it redirected my thinking outside of my own world and into someone else's. Of course I wish to this day that Brian would not have to live with ulcerative colitis, but in stepping out of my own self and serving him, I came to understand more and more that we are all here for each other. I have said before that grief can become all consuming and self-focussed. As I cared for Brian, my eyes and heart were turned further away from my own sorrow and I began to fight for his recovery.

Other friends were fighting for him too with their prayers and offers of help. One of my loveliest memories from this time is how a lady from my church sent her husband to the hospital to see us clutching a box of goodies. In it there were lovely filled bread rolls, cakes and other gifts, which I could both share with Brian and hospital staff and bring home to share with Colin for supper. It meant I didn't have to cook when I came home but instead had a picnic in the living room! The contents of this box sustained us for a couple of days and built our strength up when we needed it so much. It was such a blessing, such a lovely gesture and I remain thankful to this lady (you know who you are!) all these years later. Any good turn done for those who are suffering is never wasted and I have learned over the years that we are blessed in order that we will be a blessing to others. As God has given us His gifts, so we must pass them on to others.

'And my God will meet all your needs according to the riches of his glory in Christ Jesus.' (Philippians 4:19 NIV)

Brian and Oonagh grew in their love for each other and were married in May 2007. I am delighted to share that at the time of writing this book, they have a baby on the way!

At the point that Brian left to get married, I was both excited about the wedding and so scared about a future living on my own. The wedding day itself was beautiful and I had enjoyed myself so much, watching the happy couple start their new life together. Oddly, at the end of the day, I found I was not dreading coming home to an empty house as I thought I would be.

My friend had an overnight bag of mine in her home so I could stay with her if I wanted to, but instead I came home. As I put the key in my door and locked it behind me, I asked for God's peace to come as I knew I needed His hand to hold on this next phase of my journey through life now all the children had flown the nest.

I went to bed and slept so peacefully that night. God was holding me tenderly as He had done all my life. His peace really does surpass all understanding.

And now?

Well I keep myself busy! I work in a bustling kitchen, grateful to have regular work as it helps pay the bills. Whatever is in the future, I know that God is not finished with me yet! I want Him to use me as I testify to His faithfulness throughout the course of my life.

'No test or temptation that comes your way is beyond the course of what others have had to face. All you need to remember is that God will never let you down; He'll never let you be pushed past your limit; He'll always be there to help you come through it.' (1 Corinthians 10:13 The Message)

Not only that, but He will turn what I have gone through into good, both for me and my friends and family, and for those people I meet who are hurting too. The events that I have encountered in my life have made me into a more caring person, not afraid to go into grief situations and give whatever I can offer. It may not be much, but I do understand, and have an empathy with those who are suffering. More importantly, I know the power of prayer and how vital it is to commit everything to our loving God. Had I not had the prayers of my family and friends during the darkest times, I doubt I would have made it through. This little poem reminds me of how blessed I have been by all my friends over so many years, especially my oldest friend Jeannie:

When trouble comes your soul to try,
You love the friend who just stands by.
Perhaps there's nothing they can do
The thing is strictly up to you.
For there are troubles all your own
And paths the soul must tread alone.
Times when love can't smooth the road
Nor friendships lift the heavy load.
But just to know you have a friend
Who will stand by until the end.
Whose sympathy through all endures
Whose warm handclasp is always yours.
It helps some way to pull you through
Although there's nothing they can do,
And so with fervent heart you cry
'God bless the friend who just stands by.'

In writing this book I have come a long way. After Raymond died, I could not accept it was forever and found it hard to even say the phrase 'When Raymond died,' settling instead for 'When Raymond….' because I could not link the name of my son with death. Since the process of writing began, I can say it all and so the road to healing has reached another milestone.

God sees it all and He knows it all and I am forever grateful for His hand in my life. I may still have questions unanswered and I may feel wistful at times about how Raymond and Brian would have looked now and whether Raymond would be married with children and so on. But I am content to leave it with God, knowing that one day when I reach heaven, all things will be made complete and I will not need to know why any longer.

A relationship with God is like a lifelong friendship. We can tell Him how we feel, as we would tell our best friend; in fact He is better than a best friend! He does not need us to stand on ceremony or be religious. He simply loves to hear our heart and longs to heal our pain. It is difficult for Him to deal with our emotions unless we let Him in on them, so be full of courage and open your heart to Him today. I can honestly say you won't regret it!

'Seek the Lord while He may be found; call on Him while He is near.' (Isaiah 55:6 NIV)

8. Life in *all* its fullness!

I wanted to end this book on a practical note and so this final chapter lists ten different things that have helped me overcome the bleakness of a life of grief. I know that I will always carry the memory of those I have lost in the deepest part of my heart and that will never change.

But I am no longer weighed down under the pressure of sorrow: God has restored my joy. I am so grateful to have had my son and my husband in my life as they have made me richer, more than I can easily find the words to express here. I have journeyed through grief and loss and now find myself in a different place. I am at peace, and I have found contentment. Yes, there has been intense suffering, and I am not denying the past, but God has kindly and patiently taken my hand and led me beside quiet waters, restoring my soul in the process, as He promises in His word.

'The LORD is my shepherd; I lack nothing.
He makes me lie down in green pastures,
He leads me beside quiet waters,
He refreshes my soul.
He guides me along the right paths
for His name's sake.
Even though I walk
through the darkest valley,
I will fear no evil,
for You are with me;
Your rod and Your staff,
they comfort me.
You prepare a table before me
in the presence of my enemies.
You anoint my head with oil;
my cup overflows.
Surely Your goodness and love will follow me
all the days of my life,
and I will dwell in the house of the LORD
forever.' (Psalm 23 NIV)

God has designed life to be lived in all its fullness. Along the way, our experiences may be good or they may be bad, but the truth remains that we are made for fruitfulness and growth.

The practical nature of this chapter is intentional as I want it to help you, encourage you and bring you hope as you read. You may not be ready to implement some or even any of these suggestions right now, or you may find other things that suit you better in time, but if my words can encourage just one person reading them, I will have accomplished my task! My experiences of life will not be the same as yours, and vice versa, but we share the universal truth that are all made in Gods image, whether we know Him or not. He created us to live in the richness of life and so let me tell you what has worked for me as I have journeyed with Him through the years.

Walking

When I was right in the middle of the raw grief, I used to walk for survival, pounding the hills and fields to clear my head. It was therapy for me then and it still is today. I live beside a glen that the council were working on when Raymond died and which was formally opened to the public during the month of his death. It was then, and still is, a very soothing place for me since some of the spaces are wide open and some are enclosed, meaning that there is a change of light and sound as I move from one place to the other. Bluebells grow there in abundance in the spring and the colours of every season are stunning. In the summer the glen waterfall is a trickle, but in the winter it gushes with clear water from higher ground.

I go to the glen when my thoughts are all over the place and over the years I have left a lot of anger there amongst the trees. Now that I am much more at peace in myself, I believe there is ongoing healing to be found in walking and exercise. I have joined a walking club and I have met some lovely people who get together every other week for a good day out. We walk from early morning to late afternoon, taking a picnic lunch with us. Sometimes we go away for a whole weekend which will have been organized for us which is brilliant for me as all I have to do is just turn up! We have an annual Christmas dinner and dance night too, which is always great fun.

We are a mixed group of people from all walks of life, and no one is interested in delving deep into private matters with anyone else. The common ground is a love of walking and that is how it remains. Small talking while walking is one of the most soothing things I do and can be more healing than people expect. In fact, one of my friends went through a tragic life event some years ago and she came walking with me, only to find that it helped to heal her broken heart. Wonderful.

Taking care of myself

After Raymond died I don't remember my appearance being an issue. I lost a lot of weight and probably bought smaller clothes perhaps, but after Brian died, how I looked became very important to me because he wasn't there to hide behind any more.

Even though I have always liked how I look and have never really had an image issue as some do, nevertheless after Brian died I felt I had to dress the best I could to keep my self-image healthy. I resolved to keep my hair neat and not let the grey hairs take over until I was ready!

Years ago, widows wore black but after Brian died I never did. Wearing black didn't make me grieve Brian more and, in fact, I think dark clothes would have made me feel worse. Bright coloured clothes made me feel good, and sometimes they could significantly lift my mood on the mornings I awoke feeling bleak. Even when I did not feel like dressing well, I made a choice to take myself in hand and decide to make the effort even when sometimes it was very difficult.

I wear a bit of make up because it is an enhancement to what we already have! In my experience, once the initial weeks of grief were over, and I entered the next stages of acceptance that my loved ones were not coming back, I began to think a little more clearly and resume the usual routines which included wearing make up.

I certainly never did this in order to impress anyone: I did it to regain some normality and order into my world that felt like it had spiralled out of control. Grief has to be lived through, but it does not have to take control, so choosing to return to one or two normal routines is a good thing.

Trips away

Every year, in December or January, I go away with about eight close friends for a two-night stay in a hotel. We try and work it so that everyone is free to come and it is always the best therapy for all of us. We laugh together, chat, shop, walk, take photographs, enjoy good food and sometimes take time to talk seriously about our respective lives.

These weekends are so important for us all. They give us an opportunity to recharge our batteries and take some time away from the familiar surroundings of home. I can't recommend this type of venture highly enough.

Yes, they require some planning and timetables need to be juggled, but it is so worth it for the rest, fun, relationship building and recuperation. I have never failed to return home refreshed and every one my friends would say the same.

If going away with as many as eight other people is not your idea of fun, perhaps you could go away with one or two friends instead. The social dynamic may be different (it will be quieter for one thing!) but the effects are the same.

There was a time I could not have imagined enjoying something like this, and may even have felt guilty for considering it, given all the sorrow in and around me. If you feel this way, my advice is to take your time and don't rush it. You may not be ready right now, but one day you will be, so have it as a plan for the future.

Books and television

In the first few years after the deaths of Raymond and Brian, I could not have read a book or watched TV if you had paid me, because everything would remind me of my own life. If I saw a news report about a mother and a son, I would go back into my own journey. If I read an article about loneliness I would feel myself descend into darkness that threatened to overwhelm me. Grief draws us into ourselves and when we are journeying through it, it is the filter through which we view life.

We ache with it and it is common to find that we need to identify with others going through it to keep it alive. But this is not always helpful as it can transfer over into self-indulgence, so it is better to steer clear of visual images or stories and articles that feed the emotions unnecessarily.

After a few years I found I could read a short story in a magazine, and eventually as I healed I could begin to watch television. In those days I could maybe get through a whole film without thinking about anything to do with my own life, and now it is absolutely fine as I am able to watch programmes for what they are.

I happily read books now and I have discovered that they do help me a great deal. All through my life I have loved reading true stories about the lives of others, and now I can read autobiographies without making them try to fit my own story.

Counselling

In the early days following the passing of Raymond and Brian, I found it hard to find someone who would offer me the counselling I believe I needed to help me get through the initial phases of the loss. I think I would have benefitted as an individual and the family would also have been helped by being given the space to spill out all the emotions together in a safe, neutral environment.

We were all watching each other, and at times we were treading on eggshells to make room for each other's pain. Talking about it together may have significantly helped the healing process. My advice would be to not ignore the value of talking and praying with a qualified Christian counsellor.

Don't be frightened of pursuing the need to talk. Not everyone will want to necessarily, so try not to force it, but it will encourage those who are locked away to open up and receive healing. Counselling is appropriate for any kind of brokenness and pain and even schools these days will provide it, and it is more in vogue these days than it used to be.

A year or so after Raymond died I went on a course to become a counsellor in order to see what it could do for me and what I could learn. I did gain some understanding of how many people are hurting and how it was not just me who was broken. I learned too, how people who loved each other hurt each other and how many people are hurt by unfaithfulness in the name of love. It certainly opened my eyes.

If you do try counselling and it is not helping, defer it until another time in the future. It is not that you have failed, or your issues are too complex; it may be that just as there are times and seasons for everything, perhaps it was too soon to start. Counselling requires us to be honest and authentic with where we are at, so it takes courage to step into it. If you are not ready to expose your emotions in this way, wait awhile until you are. Nothing should be forced: remember, it is step-by-step, little by little.

Church

As I have said previously, I am a member of an active and vibrant church and I am so glad about that! Most of the people in it have, to some degree, shared my journey with me over the years and I am very thankful for it, as it has kept me walking.

Why is church so important? Well, the Bible tells us that when one suffers we all suffer because we are family, and families care about each other.

'If one part suffers, every part suffers with it; if one part is honoured, every part rejoices with it.' (1 Corinthians 12:26 NIV)

I wonder why it is that when we are suffering, we can so easily withdraw from our church family? Maybe we feel that people are watching us, judging us, or failing to understand our predicament. The irony is that it is actually better for us to be in a loving community when we are suffering rather than outside it. If you feel like withdrawing from church, ask a trusted friend or pastor to keep praying for you.

Even if you don't think that prayer is working for you or you doubt that God understands or even cares about what you are going through, ask someone to commit to praying for you until you work through it. I had so much anger and bitterness in me after Raymond died, that it nearly destroyed me. I had to work through it because it had taken hold of me, and was destroying me by seeping into every aspect of my life and relationships. God has taken my anger away and He can do that for you too. I have to say, I am a much better person without it!

Initially it was difficult going back to church after Raymond died, as I hadn't been very often for about twenty years. For instance, whilst I loved singing the songs and hymns, they would make me cry which could be embarrassing at times. Thankfully, people understood and kindly let me encounter God in my own way, letting the music and words wash my soul, bringing me joy as I healed deep down. So too, the words of the preaching kept me full of hope and rooted in truth when everything around me was a swirling tornado.

My church is an expression of God to me, and it is like my extended family where I am nurtured, cared for, prayed for and generally looked after. And I do the same for others in return.

There is no perfect church, but since it is the Body of Christ on earth, within it you will find grace, mercy and love shown in other people as they live out the message of the gospel. What a wonderful, healing place to be!

Prayer group

I believe that being part of a smaller prayer group is also very important. It is not necessary to feel or act super spiritual to join one, as the best groups will be those where honesty, love and loyalty to one another are cherished and valued. Neither should it matter if we don't like to, want to, or know how to pray out loud in a group such as this.

The crucial thing is to feel welcomed into a body of people who will commit to praying for each other through whatever life throws at them, without any judgement, pressure or expectation. In a crisis, it is wonderful to be only a phone call away from a group of friends who you know will talk to God on your behalf, praying the prayers that you need and perhaps have no strength to say yourself.

Of course, it is not just in the crises that prayer group's function well. They are places to celebrate when God answers the prayers prayed together, whether it is for salvation of a loved one, success in a job interview or the restoration of a relationship that had previously been broken.

I believe 100% in the power of prayer. I can testify to the truth of the promise in the Bible that prayer does indeed change things and God actually wants us to talk to Him. The Apostle Paul says,

'Do not be anxious about anything, but in every situation, by prayer and petition, with thanksgiving, present your requests to God.' (Philippians 4:6 NIV)

so if you are not part of one already, form or join an existing prayer group and you will see the benefit it offers you again and again.

Verses around the house

During the times when I experienced the most desperate grief, I would never have been able to read long chapters of the Bible and certainly never done an in depth study of it. However, I did understand that I still needed the truth from God's word to sink into my heart and feed my soul, especially as my mind was preoccupied with other things. The Bible is not just for head knowledge; it is *'God-breathed'* (2 Timothy 3:16 NIV) and when we read it, something like the breath of God fills our whole self and changes our perspectives on life.

With my emotions stretched to breaking point on so many occasions, I would stop to read the verses I had left around the rooms of the house and be comforted in the deepest ways. I would pray that the children would also be blessed as they saw them and read them when they wanted to.

Some verses were promises,

'Call to me and I will answer you and tell you great and unsearchable things you do not know.' (Jeremiah 33:3 NIV)

Some were encouragements,

'Do not let your hearts be troubled. You believe in God believe also in Me.' (John 14:1 NIV)

And some were sayings, based on the truth of the word similar to this one, which I have in my home to this day.

'God has not promised sun without rain, joy without sorrow, peace without pain. But God has promised strength for the day, rest for the labour, light for the way, grace for the trials, help from above, unfailing sympathy, undying love.' (Anon)

God is patient and does not give us tomorrow's grace, today. He gives us enough for each day so try not to worry about how you will feel tomorrow, just focus on each day as it comes.

Charity work

Once the raw pain begins to abate, I firmly believe that looking outside of your own context is a very good thing. That is why I became involved in a charity called 'Project Romania' which is headed up by a lovely couple called Norman and Linda Patterson.

As these things often do, my involvement came about through a friend, Liz, who had previously heard Linda speak about her passion for the Romanian gypsy community. Liz invited me and some friends Pearl, Lynda and Paula to join her in making cards once a week that we sell, giving all the proceeds to the charity. Once a year, at Christmas time, Liz hosts a coffee morning in her home where we sell jewellery made by her daughter, the cards we have crafted, homemade cakes and other items. Over the years we have been able to give what I hope is a significant donation to help towards the building of houses for the Romanian families who have no home of their own. The houses built by the charity are simple and basic but provide shelter, warmth and, very importantly, a sense of belonging.

Through my connection with the charity, I have visited Romania three times for about 10 days at a time, and each time I have considered it a privilege to meet the people we are helping. I was both shocked by the poverty and blessed by the people. In some ways, it was like stepping back to what Ireland was like hundreds of years ago. When I saw things first hand the first time I went, I felt a burden for the suffering and hurting of our world.

I remember being so moved as I dressed a little gypsy girl in a new outfit we had taken out, throwing away her worn out rags and watching her smile from ear to ear as she paraded around in her new clothes. Supporting charities from the comfort of our own armchair is good, but travelling to meet the people themselves is even better. For me, helping the poor first hand has meant that I have identified with the compassion of Jesus in a deeper way. It has challenged so many of my pre-conceived ideas and given me a better understanding of the whole Gospel. My prayer is that in reading about my own experiences, you will be encouraged to do the same: it really is worth it!

Family

I love my family: they give me so much joy! When I look at them all, I no longer see what we have lost, but what we have gained over the years of walking together through life. I am not incomplete through loss but complete in God, and I am so thankful to Him for each and every member of this family of mine, including those who are no longer with us. God has given me a rich life, full of the depth and breadth of His love and grace. Now when I remember Raymond and Brian, I can only bring myself to thank Him for giving them to us all and for the years they lived with us.

In the eyes of my grandchildren I see an innocence that warms me. As I pray for them, I pray that they will never have to walk my journey, but even so, I know that my God is their God and He will be just as faithful throughout their lives and guide them in the choices they make.

Conclusion

We all have storms in our lives. It is understandable that we can sometimes lose our perspective when we are buffeted by tragic events, but God has promised in His word that when the storms come, He will rebuild us.

'Afflicted city, lashed by storms and not comforted, I will rebuild you with stones of turquoise, your foundations with lapis lazuli.'
(Isaiah 54:11 NIV)

God does not stop the storms happening, but He is right there in the middle of them with us, whether we feel His presence or not. Why? Well, because He is a loving Father.

Whatever place you are in today as you finish reading this book, my prayer is that you will remember that the God is near. My experience of Him is that no matter how far we are from Him, or what life throws at us, His presence remains with us because He loves us. That is the message of the cross; that Jesus would pay the ultimate price to make the way clear for a deep, full, rich, honest and authentic relationship with Him.

In the complex depths of the human experience, we have a choice. We can rage against God forever, or we can choose to begin to walk with Him, authentically, trusting that whatever the journey holds, He will be with us every step and one day we will look back, as I have, and be thankful. I didn't always make the 'right' choices in the early days but God has always loved me as He has always loved you. So don't give up! Keep it real with God and your loved ones and hold on tight. You may feel shattered, but in God, you are never broken beyond His repair.

Prayer
You may have come to a place now where you want to recommit your ways to God, giving Him the permission to lead you into more of His love and grace. The Bible says

'Seek the Lord while he may be found; call on Him while He is near.' (Isaiah 55:6 NIV)

So in the quietness and peace now, I want to invite you to pray this prayer:

'Lord, I give you my heart. There is no one else who can love me and heal me like you can, so I am calling on you to come and walk with me on my journey through life. I know you have always loved me and always will, even in the times when I have been angry with you, rejected you, ignored you, or been unable to feel your presence. Thank you for loving me like that, and for the mercy that is given to me through the work of the cross. Thank you that with you I can be real so I don't have to pretend. You take me as I am, and I am so grateful. So I am inviting you into my life, knowing that day by day, you will change me so that I reflect more of your glory and grace to all those I meet.'

In Jesus' name
Amen.

Colin & Cherry's kids

Shane & Tracy's kids

Sheena & Nigel's kids